W9-AGH-992

30 SECOND
MYSTERIES
CASE FILES

spinner books

San Francisco • Maastricht • Sydney

Warning: Small parts may be a choking hazard. Not for children under 3 years.

ACKNOWLEDGEMENTS

Special thanks to Bob Lindstrom and Kristen Schoen.

Designers: Andis Lindbergs and Jeanette Miller

30 Second Mysteries: Case Files, Spinner Books and The Book You Can Play!
are all trademarks of University Games. Copyright © 2006 by University
Games Corporation, San Francisco, CA 94110. All Rights Reserved.

No part of this book may be used or reproduced in any
manner whatsoever without the written permission of the Publisher.

University Games Europe B.V., Australiëlaan 52,
6199 AA Maastricht Airport, Netherlands.

University Games Australia, 10 Apollo Street, Warriewood, Australia 2102.

Retain this information for future reference.

ISBN 1-57528-880-X

Printed in Mexico

07 08 09 10 11 RRD 9 8 7 6 5 4 3

CONTENTS

INTRODUCTION

Jeff Pinsker and I co-developed dozens of games together, but none were as challenging or memorable as *30 Second Mysteries*. What a story! Jeff and I decided to invent the ultimate party game for the witty and the precocious. We wanted the game to be quick, tricky, educational and fun. We came up with the title *30 Second Mysteries* – and the notion that if players were clever they could solve the mysteries in 30 seconds, and if we were clever we could write them in 30 seconds.

Jeff and I met one snowy day in London at the John Bull Pub to turn our concept into reality. We sat for nearly nine hours and created the game as we consumed one fine British lager after another. The results of our day in London were collected in the first volume of *30 Second Mysteries*. Since then we have added two more volumes.

Each 30 second mystery is a fun, interactive form of a good old-fashioned whodunit. This collection has all our classics, from volumes I and II, and 56 new cases to entertain you, your friends and your colleagues for hours. It's sure to exercise your logical and critical thinking muscles, as well as tease your funny bone.

We had a great time putting these mysteries together and hope you have even more fun trying to solve them.

Good Luck!

Bob Moog

RULES

OBJECT

To be the first player or team to solve 7 mysteries or score 7 points.

PLAYING THE GAME

• First things first: grab a pen and paper to keep track of your points.

• The youngest player spins first to determine the type of mystery to be solved (i.e. Who, What, Where or Why) and reads the first Case and Mystery from that category out loud to the group. This player acts solely as a reader and may not play until the mystery is solved. The player to the left of the Reader gets the first clue—and the first stab at solving the mystery.

• *If a player guesses the mystery incorrectly (or doesn't have a guess),* the player to his/her left gets the next clue and may then try to crack the case. Play proceeds in a clockwise fashion.

• *If a player guesses the mystery correctly,* s/he earns a point and the player to the Reader's left becomes the new Reader for the next case in the same category. Do not spin again until each player has read a mystery to the group.

• Once all players have acted as the Reader, it is time to spin again! The player to the left of the last person to spin now spins to determine the type of mystery to be solved. S/he is the first reader for this round.

• *Tip:* Don't forget to jot down the number of the last mystery solved in case you spin the same category more than once, which is likely to happen.

SCORING

The first player to guess the mystery scores 1 point. If a player solves the mystery without hearing any clues, s/he earns 2 points.

WINNING THE GAME

The first player to score 7 points wins!

PLAYING ON YOUR OWN

Spin and read The Case and The Mystery question from the appropriate category. Try to solve the case using as few clues as possible.

SCORING:

10 points = 0 clues revealed

6 points = 1 clue revealed

5 points = 2 clues revealed

4 points = 3 clues revealed

3 points = 4 clues revealed

2 points = 5 clues revealed

1 point = 6 clues revealed

0 points = Incorrect guess!

Read 10 mysteries. Collect 40 points or more and you're a winner!

WHO

CASE 1

THE CASE

A young boy arrives by train to his new school. The school is the best of its kind, but it doesn't appear on any map, nor does it appear on any list of best schools. The school is British, but is not actually in Britain. The school's fame has spread to the United States through a series of literary efforts that describe the activities of the school's unique curriculum and student body.

THE MYSTERY

What is the name of the school and who is its most famous student?

THE CLUES

The school is actually a converted castle.
The school is a boarding school that takes seven years to complete.
An owl is the school's official mascot.
The school's students don't use brooms for sweeping.
J. K. Rowling brought the school to life in her series of best-selling books.

CASE 2

THE CASE

An alcoholic recluse who lives far from the limelight goes into his workplace. He refuses to work in what could be considered "normal" ways, instead preferring to kneel on the floor while he labors. Because of his unique approach, he gains national and then international acclaim, but sabotages his health and dies tragically in the end.

THE MYSTERY

Who was this man and why was he famous?

THE CLUES

The man was American.
A car crash took his life.
The man smoked and drank to excess.
A biopic of his life was released starring Ed Harris.
The man was nicknamed "Jack the Dripper."

WHO

CASE 3

THE CASE
A famous man has plotted the deaths of well over a hundred people, many of whom were royalty. Some survived, but many did not. The man is famous the world over for what he's done—yet he's never been tried in a court of law.

THE MYSTERY
Who were the man's two most famous victims and what was the man's name?

THE CLUES
The man killed his victims with his bare hands.
The man is deceased.
The man was English and lived in the 16th century.
The victims were star-crossed lovers.
The man knew that the pen is mightier than the sword.

CASE 4

WHO

THE CASE
In the late 1960s, a person not known as a professional athlete performs a sporting feat for the first time in recorded history. Thousands of other people would be better at performing the feat than this person, yet the media covers the event and millions of people watch.

THE MYSTERY
Who was the person and where was the sport played?

THE CLUES
The sport is played by millions of people.
The person is a man who works for the government.
The man is a celebrated American pilot.
The sport requires a good swing.
The man played in outer space.

CASE 5

THE CASE

In the middle of the afternoon, a woman finds a hidden key and unlocks the door to a house she's never seen. She takes notes and photos of everything she sees but nothing else. She leaves the house as quietly as she entered.

THE MYSTERY

Who is the woman and why has she entered the house?

THE CLUES

The woman is not a friend or relative of the owners.
The owners of the house were expecting the woman, but had hidden the key.
The woman has a contract with the homeowner.
The woman knows how valuable the house is.
The woman makes homes her business.

CASE 6

THE CASE

Despite international recognition, a well-known King never wore a crown or a robe and was not considered royalty in his native land. He was both loved and hated and could not be deterred from trying to rise up against the injustices in his land.

THE MYSTERY

Who was the man and what year did he die?

THE CLUES

He did not have a Roman numeral after his name.
He shared his name with his father.
The nation mourned his death.
He was a doctor, but he never went to medical school.
He died in April in Tennessee.

CASE 7

THE CASE
A person has the same job for years. The person enjoys his work, but spends most days staring at the ceiling. Despite this behavior, his work turns out to be among the most important ever done in his field.

THE MYSTERY
Who is the person and what did the person do?

THE CLUES
The person was left hanging for much of the job.
The person was Italian.
The person was born in the 15th century.
The person was a man—and is usually known by his first name.
The man worked on the ceiling of a famous chapel.

CASE 8

THE CASE
Parents willingly take their children to visit an eccentric middle-aged man in his extravagant residence. They do not know the man and are anxious about entering his home. Once inside, they must save their children from near disaster as a result of their affiliations with this man. Still, he is never charged with a single crime.

THE MYSTERY
Who is the man and where does he live?

THE CLUES
The man likes his sweets.
The children are all contest winners.
The man offers the parents and their kids a sweet deal.
Roald Dahl wrote a book about the man.
The man is also known as the Candy Man.

CASE 9

THE CASE

A man spends much of his day indoors, peering through Windows. The man is not considered a recluse—rather, he has built an impressive organization, attracted a huge number of followers and amassed great wealth. Although his organization has been under investigation by the U.S. government, many of his followers believe the man has changed their lives.

THE MYSTERY

Who is the man and what is the name of his organization?

THE CLUES

The man is considered a revolutionary and has followers all over the world.
The organization's materials can be found in homes throughout the U.S.
The man was born in the 1950s.
The organization is in the "high tech" sector.
The man is one of the wealthiest people in America.

CASE 10

THE CASE

A patriot travels on a small horse to a faraway village. Upon arriving, he places part of a nearby bird into his clothing. He then appears quite confused by pronouncing to all within earshot that he has in his possession some Italian pasta.

THE MYSTERY

Who is the patriot and what is the Italian pasta?

THE CLUES

He is visiting a city on the East Coast.
Most people learn about him even before they enter school.
He was popular during the forming of our nation.
His name identifies him as a Northerner.
His story is continually repeated in song.

WHO

CASE 11

THE CASE

A masked man calmly and quietly approaches a young woman. The woman kneels and begs the masked man to leave her alone. Her husband does nothing to intervene, even though he could easily stop her from being harmed. Although the masked man's identity is known, he is not arrested, even after he kills the woman.

THE MYSTERY

Who was the woman and what was her husband's name?

THE CLUES

The woman was 29 when she died.
The woman lived on an island.
The masked man was paid for what he did.
The woman was part of the British royal family.
The husband had many wives and ordered the woman beheaded.

CASE 12

THE CASE

Two men dressed in dark clothing enter a wealthy neighborhood in the early morning hours. They move quickly from house to house, taking everything they can. A policeman observes the pair—but does not approach or arrest them.

THE MYSTERY

Who are the men and what do they take?

THE CLUES

The men wear gloves and leave no fingerprints.
The men avoid certain houses.
The men have worked this neighborhood before and are experts at what they do.
The men aren't breaking the law.
The men come every week at the same time.

WHO

CASE 13

WHO

THE CASE

A man leaves his rowdy travel companions to seek some peace and quiet. After a long walk, he hears a voice telling him to return to his group. He returns feeling better, and carries with him some important instructions he discovered at the end of his walk. To his surprise, the rowdy group is entirely out of control and has surrounded a large farm animal.

THE MYSTERY

Who is the man and where is he?

THE CLUES

The man and his group were near a famous mountain.
The man's long walk lasted several days.
The group of people numbered in the thousands.
The farm animal was made of gold.
The country was Egypt.

CASE 14

THE CASE

A man with many aliases has an international reputation, but has never been seen. Occasionally, he dashes out under the cover of night. His home is very remote and nearly impossible to reach.

THE MYSTERY

What is the man called in the U.S. and where is his home?

THE CLUES

The man is elderly, but age doesn't slow him down.
The man usually wears a suit.
The man has never been on a plane, but has flown all over the world.
The man employs little helpers to carry out his business.
The man's favorite pet is the reindeer.

CASE 15

THE CASE

A man stretches as far as he can to save a woman from falling fifty feet below, but misses. Without a scratch on her body, the woman stands up and walks away smiling.

THE MYSTERY

Who is the woman and why does she survive the fall unscathed?

THE CLUES

A crowd watches the accident nervously but does nothing to help.
Even though the man fails to catch her, she does not hold a grudge.
The woman's life is never truly in any danger.
The woman works hard for a living, but is a real swinger.
The woman performs under a big tent.

CASE 16

THE CASE

With no apparent motive, a young man commits a savage attack in his neighborhood. The man's community knows about the incident, but cannot implicate him. The man's conscience eats at him until he confesses and turns himself in for punishment.

THE MYSTERY

Who is the man and what weapon did he use in his attack?

THE CLUES

The police were not involved and no blood appeared on the weapon.
The man led many more attacks in his career.
The man went on to become a famous "father".
The weapon was used in his family's backyard.
The man has a U.S. city named after him.

CASE 17

THE CASE

Anthony's wife has not been speaking to him lately. Anthony comes home early from work and sees an unfamiliar car in the driveway. He anxiously opens the door and finds his wife with another man. Anthony is startled, but says nothing and fixes himself a snack.

THE MYSTERY

Who was the man and why hadn't Anthony's wife been speaking to him?

THE CLUES

The man in the house was not a stranger.
The man in the house was carrying the tools of his trade.
Anthony's wife had been sick for several days.
Anthony's wife was fully clothed.
Anthony was hoping the man would get his wife to talk to him again.

CASE 18

THE CASE

A man works with the police to identify criminals. His help is invaluable even when he hasn't witnessed the crime. Many of the criminals he identifies are never caught, but the police continue to ask the man for help. Coincidentally, the man's first name describes what he does to help the police.

THE MYSTERY

What is the man's first name and what is his occupation?

THE CLUES

The man's name is not unusual.
The man is on the police payroll.
The man works with his hands and listens carefully to what other people have to say.
The man is a trained professional, but also draws on his natural talent.
The man has a three-letter name.

WHO

CASE 19

THE CASE
Every day of his life a fellow confronts danger, often finding himself facing the barrel of a gun. With keen acuity, he's able to escape every time, sometimes by dodging bullets or romancing his foe, and always by poking fun at others.

THE MYSTERY
Who is this rascal and what is his favorite catchphrase?

THE CLUES
He lives underground.
Kids have enjoyed him for generations.
He hangs around with some real loonies.
His favorite food is carrots.
Though not a physician, he often refers to his adversary as one.

CASE 20

WHO

THE CASE
A throng of onlookers scream when an unknown man turns on a machine. $33\frac{1}{2}$ hours later, he turns the machine off and is an instant celebrity. He hasn't slept or had any visitors—but is now in a foreign country.

THE MYSTERY
Who is the man and what is his machine called?

THE CLUES
The man is known for being a loner.
The machine hangs in the Smithsonian Institution.
The machine is an airplane.
The man became famous in 1927 and is known for his spirit.
The man was involved in a famous kidnapping.

CASE 21

THE CASE

Laurel lives a peaceful life in a wooded region of the United States. One day, a person approaches and savagely attacks Laurel with a sharp weapon. Laurel is mortally wounded and dies. The person sells Laurel's body for a good price.

THE MYSTERY

Who was Laurel and why did the person sell Laurel's body?

THE CLUES

Laurel was tall and slender.
Laurel had a quiet disposition and a sweet smell.
Although Laurel was cut with an axe, there was no blood.
Laurel's body was cut into pieces before it was sold.
Laurel is not a person.

CASE 22

THE CASE

As part of his job, a man climbs a ladder, gets caught in a windstorm and ends up trapped inside a glass booth. Some people see him struggling and offer money; others turn their backs and walk away. The man never asks for help and no one makes any effort to help him.

THE MYSTERY

What is the man's occupation and who pays him?

THE CLUES

The man's job requires training.
The man wears the same outfit to work every day.
Some laugh at the man's struggles.
The man relies on the kindness of strangers.
The man wears black and white makeup to work.

WHO

CASE 23

THE CASE

A person tries for years to get the financial backing needed for a commercial venture. After finally finding a backer, the person buys materials, hires employees and begins work. The venture doesn't meet its objective, but the person's efforts change the world and the backers are elated by the results.

THE MYSTERY

Who was the person and what year was the venture launched?

THE CLUES

The person was an Italian male.
The venture used existing technology in a new way.
The man's financial backers were Spanish.
The objective of the venture was to explore new territory.
The venture began near the end of the 15th century.

CASE 24

THE CASE

A car pulls up the driveway of Mr. & Mrs. Stone. A stranger gets out of the car and rings the doorbell. Mrs. Stone peeks through the curtains and yells for her teenage daughter Vickie to stay upstairs. Mr. Stone opens the door and he and the stranger talk in hushed voices. The stranger is let inside and asks for Vickie. As Mr. Stone goes to get the girl, Mrs. Stone starts to cry.

THE MYSTERY

Who is the stranger and where does he plan to take Vickie?

THE CLUES

Mr. Stone told the stranger to take care of Vickie.
Mrs. Stone cautions Vickie to be careful.
Mr. & Mrs. Stone can't believe this is happening.
It is May and Vickie is a senior in high school.
Mr. & Mrs. Stone take a picture for posterity's sake and tell Vickie they'll see her at midnight.

WHO

CASE 25

WHO

THE CASE
A man and his family live in a large metropolitan area. They neither own a house nor pay rent. As long as the family qualifies, they are allowed to live in housing subsidized by the government.

THE MYSTERY
Who is the family and where do they live?

THE CLUES
The house is in America.
The house could be called a "country" house.
The number of family members usually changes at least once a decade.
One family member works for the government—and is a public figure.
The family lives in the nation's capital.

WHO

CASE 26

THE CASE
A man finds himself surrounded by hostile strangers who literally want a piece of him. He flees, but encounters fierce animals and natural obstacles. Finally, he places his trust in a friendly stranger, only to be betrayed and murdered.

THE MYSTERY
Who is the man and who betrays him?

THE CLUES
The man is fond of speaking in rhymes.
He can't swim, but the friendly stranger can.
Before his escape, the man is kept in an oven.
The friendly stranger is known for his clever and foxy demeanor.
The man is irresistibly sweet.

WHO

CASE 27

THE CASE

A man with a desk job habitually responds to emergencies. He provides his own uniform and performs these civic deeds entirely on a voluntary basis.

THE MYSTERY

Who is the man and what is on the front of his uniform?

THE CLUES

The man was adopted and given a new name by his parents.
The man changes clothes in many different places.
The man is a journalist.
The man's uniform is primarily blue—and very well fitted.
The man can leap tall buildings in a single bound.

CASE 28

THE CASE

An extremely muscular young man in excellent health goes to bed with his girlfriend one night. When he wakes up the next morning he is still healthy, but has lost a lot of his strength. A short time later, he commits a terrorist act, taking his own life and thousands of others in the process.

THE MYSTERY

Who is the man and what was the key to his strength?

THE CLUES

The man's physical strength stemmed from his spiritual strength.
The man's physical appearance was altered while he slept.
The man is part of a famous pair.
The man prayed and regained his strength one last time.
The man's strength was cut short by the woman who betrayed him.

WHO

CASE 29

THE CASE

A man builds a castle but never lives in it, despite its popularity. Even after his death, millions pay homage every year, encountering enormous beasts and witnessing terrible explosions. Though exhausted and drained of valuable resources, many feel compelled to make another pilgrimage to the castle's grounds in the future.

THE MYSTERY

Who built the castle and where is it?

THE CLUES

A TV and movie producer designed the castle.
The castle is part of a magical place.
The castle is in California.
The castle is surrounded by an amusement park.
The castle's creator brought Pinocchio to life.

CASE 30

THE CASE

One day in the late 1930s, a skillful professional goes to work and never returns home. There is no sign of foul play. The authorities conduct an extensive search, but never find the person.

THE MYSTERY

What was this person's name and profession?

THE CLUES

The person was a woman who was a pioneer in her profession.
The woman was born in 1898.
The profession requires a special license.
It is presumed that the woman died, but some people are still searching for her remains today.
The woman's popularity soared to new heights after she disappeared.

CASE 31

THE CASE

One fateful day in a courthouse in the American South, a young litigator hears the disturbing tale of a girl's rape. He is so moved by the story that he changes the direction of his life permanently. From that point on, he wakes up early to pursue this new passion that will one day make him quite wealthy.

THE MYSTERY

Who is the man and what did he become?

THE CLUES

The man was a member of the Mississippi House of Representatives for seven years.
An attorney by training, the man now makes his living at a computer.
The man is one of modern publishing's great success stories.
Nearly all of the man's books have made it to the silver screen.
The man knows Tom Cruise, Julia Roberts and Susan Sarandon.

CASE 32

THE CASE

A man meets some visitors from Africa. The visitors do not speak English, seem to be friendly and are not wearing clothes. The visitors are in the country legally and have not committed a crime, but are behind bars. The man feels for the visitors, but does not try to help them escape.

THE MYSTERY

Who are the visitors and where are they behind bars?

THE CLUES

The visitors are behind bars for life.
The visitors make lots of noise.
The man pays to see the visitors.
The visitors are not people.
The visitors love bananas and are real "swingers."

CASE 33

WHO

THE CASE

Parker crouches under a table in his house, fearing for his life. His two brothers have already been attacked and he knows he may be next when the enemy finds him. Moments later, he hears his enemy taunting him, but he remains in seclusion, hoping for the best. After surviving a huge blast, Parker knows he is finally safe for good.

THE MYSTERY

Who is Parker and who is his enemy?

THE CLUES

Parker is smarter than his brothers.
Parker's enemy is large, intimidating and very hairy.
Parker's enemy has strong lungs.
Parker's house is made of brick.
Parker's enemy enjoys a good pork chop.

WHO

CASE 34

THE CASE

A bald male opens his eyes and finds himself naked in a small room full of people he doesn't recognize. A female grabs him and starts to hit him before he can utter a word. He is shocked and bursts into tears.

THE MYSTERY

Who is the male and who is the female?

THE CLUES

The female has hit other males before.
The male is not being punished.
The female is being paid to treat the male this way.
The male is getting medical treatment.
The male has no teeth.

WHO

CASE 35

THE CASE

A man screams for over an hour and wakes up the majority of people who live in his neighborhood. Rather than complain about the noise or tell the man to stop, his neighbors give him an enthusiastic response.

THE MYSTERY

Who was the man and what four words was he yelling?

THE CLUES

The man is now dead.
The man lived near Boston, but wasn't a U.S. citizen.
Legend has it that the man yelled the same words over and over again.
The man warned of an impending attack.
The man rode a horse and is revered as a hero.

CASE 36

THE CASE

A woman is a contract killer. Strangely enough, the police are not interested in arresting her. She is always invited into the very homes where her murders are scheduled to take place. Her work is conducted in front of witnesses and no one even tries to stop her from killing.

THE MYSTERY

Who is this woman and how does she kill her victims?

THE CLUES

The woman never uses a gun to kill.
Anyone can identify her by her work dress.
After a year on the job, she's likely killed thousands, maybe even millions.
She usually has to wear a mask when she is working.
She often makes repeat visits to the same house.

WHO

CASE 37

WHO

THE CASE

A young trader travels to an exotic land where he liberates a woman and an animal. A native with a very keen sense of smell chases him—and he narrowly escapes with his life.

THE MYSTERY

Who was the trader and what did he trade in order to make his journey?

THE CLUES

The trader was English and never left his homeland.
The trader was inexperienced and placed his business associates' income in jeopardy.
The trader was known by his first name—and had a giant secret.
The trader speculated in bean futures.
The trader appears in a fairy tale.

CASE 38

WHO

THE CASE

The stars of a TV show are upset that they were chosen. They will probably not be on the next episode or, if they are, it will be their last appearance. They do not audition; they are chosen by the producers and by America.

THE MYSTERY

Who are the stars and on what show are they featured?

THE CLUES

The audience doesn't vote, but the producers hope they'll call in.
The stars' actions are often reenacted.
The show is nonfiction.
The show helps a government agency do important work.
The host of the show continually asks America for its help.

WHO

CASE 39

THE CASE
A contract is taken out on Vinnie "The Blade" Martorana. When the deal is done, Vinnie is worth more dead than alive. Vinnie knows about the contract, but does not alert the police.

THE MYSTERY
Who took out the contract and why isn't Vinnie worried?

THE CLUES
Vinnie knows many secrets about the person who took out the contract.
The person has a number of business arrangements with Vinnie.
Vinnie wants to live.
Vinnie has supported the person for many years.
The person loves Vinnie and doesn't want him to die.

CASE 40

THE CASE
It was April and the sun was shining. Tens of thousands of people arrived before noon to watch the nine young men battle the monster. The uniformed employees also fought against a group of out-of-towners. While all in attendance were truly excited, they knew that they would find deep despair during the coming fall.

THE MYSTERY
Who were the employees and where were they battling the monster?

THE CLUES
The event took place in a New England city.
The employees were professional athletes.
The monster was green and very tall.
The young men hadn't been victorious in more than 50 years of trying.
The young men played baseball.

WHO

CASE 41

THE CASE

A boy enters the bedroom of a young woman and her siblings. He does not use the door to enter, even though the young woman's room is three floors up. His primary purpose is to find something he's left behind. When his business is concluded, he leaves by the same means he used to arrive.

THE MYSTERY

Who is the boy and what was he looking for?

THE CLUES

The boy is famous for his adventures.
The young woman is British.
The young woman and her siblings are little Darlings.
The boy felt as though he'd lost part of himself.
Some say the boy will never grow up.

CASE 42

THE CASE

A British subject takes a nasty tumble and is never quite the same afterwards. The subject's story is chronicled by a female poet—and becomes one of her most famous works.

THE MYSTERY

Who is the subject and what is the poet's name?

THE CLUES

Numerous books have been published in the poet's name.
The subject is male.
The subject cracked under pressure.
The poet is old and may never have existed.
The poet is known to be maternal.

CASE 43

THE CASE

A man aboard a ship near a large city is awakened by a series of explosions. Although not in peril, the man cannot sleep and makes some notes in a journal. Years later, the notes are more important than they were during the person's lifetime.

THE MYSTERY

Who was the man and what city was closest to where he was that day?

THE CLUES

The words were written in the United States.
The man was born an English citizen.
The man was anxiously awaiting sunrise.
The words were written near Fort McHenry in Maryland.
The man's song is a national anthem.

CASE 44

THE CASE

A little girl finds fame, fortune and privilege. The girl's hairstyle and endorsement of a famous ship make national news, but she also achieves important accomplishments decades later in the field of international affairs.

THE MYSTERY

Who is this very famous little girl and what famous ship did she endorse?

THE CLUES

The little girl has been a colonel, a rebel, a princess and more.
For years, women copied her hairstyle.
She is known for her singing and tap dancing.
She turned Black when she got married.
In her second career, her dimples helped advance diplomacy.

CASE 45

WHO

THE CASE

A person's efforts end up inflicting pain on millions of children around the world. Despite the children's tears, the person is hailed as a hero.

THE MYSTERY

Who was the person and what resulted from the person's efforts?

THE CLUES

The person was a man.
The man invented a process.
The man was a doctor who lived during the 20th century.
The process is a vaccine that cures a crippling disease.
The vaccine can now be taken orally.

WHO

CASE 46

THE CASE

A stranger barges into a house where two small children wait alone for their mother to come home. The children are scared, but the stranger doesn't seem to notice. Instead, this individual makes the children play games they don't want to play. Eventually the stranger leaves and, surprisingly, the police are not summoned.

THE MYSTERY

Who is the individual and who made him famous?

THE CLUES

The individual arrives wearing a hat, gloves, a bow tie and a fur coat.
The individual likes to play, even on a cold, cold, wet day.
The individual brings two Things to the house.
A famous Dr. brought him to life.
The individual speaks in rhyme.

CASE 47

THE CASE

Bill found himself in a dark place surrounded by a variety of precious metals. He'd had a very busy day. He started out at a suburban home, spent time in a taxi, visited a newsstand, went to a corner deli at lunchtime and then to a movie theatre. Bill was used to change and felt like he was surrounded by it. He didn't know where he would go tomorrow, but he would probably go alone. One was, after all, Bill's favorite number.

THE MYSTERY

Who is Bill and where is he?

THE CLUES

People can never seem to get enough of Bill.
Bill is not a living person.
Bill sometimes gets quartered, but he never dies.
Bill is made of paper.
Bill's favorite president is George Washington.

CASE 48

THE CASE

A boy kills a bear and later grows up to serve his home state in the national legislature. He returns to his Southern home, only to be summoned to travel to a desolate place to fight against foreigners. He dies there, but is honored as a hero and is best remembered for his distinctive hat.

THE MYSTERY

Who was the man and from what state did he hail?

THE CLUES

The man hailed from the "Volunteer State."
The man and his family lived in a log cabin.
Walt Disney made a movie about the man.
The man died at the Alamo in 1836.
The man wore a coonskin cap and was "King of the Wild Frontier."

CASE 49

THE CASE

A government worker is assigned to assist in making the world a better place. The man was born before 1950, but was under 35 years old when he came out of retirement in the 1990s. The man has a strong preoccupation with his attractiveness, but isn't actually attractive. He speaks with an accent, but knows English quite well.

THE MYSTERY

Who is the man and what does he do for a living?

THE CLUES

The man always gets the job done, but isn't very serious about his work.
The man is famous for his dalliances.
The man always has a cast of characters that support him.
The man has bad teeth and a dated fashion sense.
The man is groovy, baby.

CASE 50

THE CASE

One man's image has inspired many people to write songs, stories and poems. He has even compelled some to travel great distances to visit him. For as long as anyone can remember, individuals around the world have seen him on a regular basis. However, he only shows his face from a distance; when people are able to reach him, he disappears.

THE MYSTERY

Who is this man and which of his features are people able to see?

THE CLUES

He is surrounded by stars, but he's not an actor.
Ancient Greeks believed he was a woman.
Farmers, fishermen and hunters look to him for advice.
He appears ageless and timeless.
He shows himself when it gets dark out.

WHO

CASE 51

THE CASE
Diana is not a native American, but she has served in the U.S. military. She hates crime and is an outspoken advocate for women's rights and peace. Diana is an incredible athlete, but is best known for her all-American uniform. She is an expert with a rope but has never performed in a rodeo.

THE MYSTERY
Who is this woman and where is she from originally?

THE CLUES
The woman is from the Caribbean.
The woman fights crime in her community and has been on TV.
The woman possesses super-human strength.
The woman was introduced in comic books.
Diana Prince is the woman's birth name.

CASE 52

THE CASE
A man walks into a room and people immediately start screaming at him. The man begs the mob not to be mean and tries to calm them by discussing his footwear. The mob continues to scream. He leaves after a few hours, but the crowd disperses only after being reassured that he has gone for good.

THE MYSTERY
Who is the man and why has the mob gathered?

THE CLUES
The man has never been in jail.
The man is used to being yelled at.
The man has a soothing voice and a commanding presence.
The man is famous for his moves, among other things.
The man is a king but does not wear a crown.

WHO

CASE 53

THE CASE

A man walks into a home with a snake and goes to the bathroom. The owner frets and hovers while the man wrestles with the snake behind closed doors. The man exits the house a half hour later, fatigued and sweaty, but victorious. The owner breathes a sigh of relief and gives the man a large sum of money for his efforts.

THE MYSTERY

Who is the man and what has he done?

THE CLUES

The man works hard for a living.
The man sometimes discovers small valuable goods while he works.
The man helps clear things up for people.
The man uses the snake as a tool.
The man likes a good pipe, but he doesn't smoke.

CASE 54

THE CASE

After taking a bad fall, a lost and bewildered young girl suspects she may have been drugged. The girl stumbles upon wild rabbits and a mischievous cat while trying to find her way. She meets many other animated characters and narrowly escapes with her life.

THE MYSTERY

Who is the girl and where has she found herself?

THE CLUES

The girl's ordeal began after a nap on the lawn.
Though she is lost and confused, she goes to a party.
She is encouraged to drink a strange brew, which has a disturbing effect on her.
The girl is quite a character.
Lewis Carroll is responsible for the girl's many adventures.

WHO

CASE 55

THE CASE

A man in handcuffs stands on a bridge surrounded by a large crowd of people. Suddenly, the man leaps off the bridge into the cold, fast-moving river below. Oddly enough, he does not drown, but climbs out of the river safe and sound and is met by an applauding crowd.

THE MYSTERY

Who was this man and why did he leap into the river wearing handcuffs?

THE CLUES

The people watching knew that the man was going to jump into the river.
Some people were surprised that the man escaped; others expected it.
The man had done similar things before.
The man was a professional magician.
The man died in 1926.

CASE 56

THE CASE

A woman sits in a dark room furiously washing her hands. She looks terribly upset and has a crazed look in her eye. There is a man and another woman in the room with her, and they listen to the woman's almost unintelligible ramblings with horror.

THE MYSTERY

Who is this woman and what is she trying to wash off her hands?

THE CLUES

The woman is a Lady, but not a tramp.
The woman is upset because she is overcome by guilt about something she and her husband have done.
Her hands are not dirty.
She will eventually die by her own hand.
The woman and her husband are characters in a famous tragedy about greed and ambition.

WHO

35

CASE 57

WHO

THE CASE

An older lady is kept in dark seclusion for days as a time. When she is allowed out, it is almost always in the morning. She is never fed. Although she is famous and loved by many, no one objects to her treatment.

THE MYSTERY

Who is the older lady and why does no one object?

THE CLUES

The lady is famous for her sweetness.
The lady always wears a collared dress and apron.
The lady is in her forties.
The lady's favorite meal is breakfast.
The lady is made of glass and her apron is a label.

WHO

CASE 58

THE CASE

A father tenderly cares for his child after its mother has left the two of them. For many months, he protects the child from a dangerous environment, sacrificing his well-being in the process. Eventually, the mother returns and the father immediately goes off to sea, leaving his child behind.

THE MYSTERY

Who is the father and where does he live?

THE CLUES

While the father does go off to sea, he's no sailor.
Without the father, the child would die almost instantly.
The father lives with many other fathers, all in a similar situation.
The mother left for many months but the father expected her return.
The father wears only a tuxedo, but is not human.

WHO

CASE 59

THE CASE

A talented entertainer gathers several of his friends and his glamorous girlfriend together to make a major motion picture. In it, he performs a new song about a colorful object in the sky, which becomes an instant national hit. The star is more famous than ever before, but never receives a penny of the millions in proceeds.

THE MYSTERY

Who is the star and who is his girlfriend?

THE CLUES

The year is 1979.
The song is considered dreamy.
The star hosts a weekly TV show with celebrity guests.
The star's girlfriend wears a blonde wig.
The star's favorite color is green.

CASE 60

THE CASE

A man enters a room where a bald man begins talking to him and asking personal questions. The man with no hair then introduces a room full of beautiful models. One by one, the women leave. As each leaves, the bald man offers money for the man to leave, as well. After one hour, the man leaves with $1 million.

THE MYSTERY

Who is the bald man and why did the man win $1 million?

THE CLUES

26 models enter the room silently.
The bald man is in his 40s and has shaved his head.
The entire event is filmed and televised by NBC and hosted by the bald man.
To receive the $1 million, the man has to be lucky with numbers.
The event took place after January 2006.

WHO

CASE 61

THE CASE

While taking a midnight stroll, Marvin is viciously attacked. After quickly rubbing something all over his body, the attackers flee. His assailants don't have weapons, but Marvin has definitely lost some blood.

THE MYSTERY

Who is attacking Marvin and what substance drives them away?

THE CLUES

At night, it is almost impossible to see the attackers.
Marvin killed a few of them with his bare hands.
Though Marvin can't press charges, he's itching for revenge.
He bought the protective substance at a drug store.
His attackers didn't kick or punch, but they did a lot of biting.

CASE 62

THE CASE

In a packed theatre, an assistant leads a physically challenged man to a seat in the middle of a stage. The man begins to move his head in an odd, irregular fashion as he performs. Instead of being put off by his behavior, the audience is in awe of what he can do and starts to applaud.

THE MYSTERY

Who is the man and what's he doing on the stage?

THE CLUES

A piano is part of his performance.
The man has been performing for 40 years.
He often wears sunglasses.
Motown gave him his start.
When he was young, "Little" preceded his name.

WHO

CASE 63

THE CASE

Deep in the woods, a portly and unassuming fellow ambles along humming to himself. He finds a large hole in the ground, which he figures must house some animal, maybe a rabbit. He squirms into the hole, but on the way back out manages to get quite stuck because of his formidable girth. Finally, a little boy comes along and rescues him by pulling him out.

THE MYSTERY

Who is this individual and where does he live?

THE CLUES

He's from Great Britain.
When he wears clothes at all, he usually just sports a t-shirt.
He feels most at home in the woods.
His favorite food is honey.
A diminutive pig is his best friend.

CASE 64

THE CASE

Two young European children ventured into the woods with nothing more than a piece of bread. One day later, they emerged with stories of attempted murder, stolen property and child abuse.

THE MYSTERY

Who were the children?

THE CLUES

The event took place several hundred years ago.
The children were siblings.
They met a woman who invited them to dinner.
The children were not very experienced in orienteering.
The children discovered an edible house during their adventure.

WHO

CASE 65

WHO

THE CASE

A young woman believes that she has heard the divine word and commences to rally her community against its chosen leaders. She becomes a symbol of freedom and conviction, but meets a violent end before her mission is fully realized. Despite her inauspicious demise, she remains a holy hero to many and is remembered for centuries.

THE MYSTERY

Who was the woman and where was she from?

THE CLUES

The woman started to gain fame while in her teens.
The woman lived in the 15th century.
The woman was not a fan of the English.
The woman is best known by her first name.
The woman was declared a Saint in 1920.

WHO

CASE 66

THE CASE

A woman sits in an old cabin without any indoor plumbing or electricity, trying desperately to do some meaningful volunteer work. Working only by candlelight, she searches her mind to develop an inspirational message to encourage a small group of revolutionary insurgents. She successfully communicates her inspirational message and her revolutionaries achieve their independent dreams.

THE MYSTERY

Who was the woman and what was the result of her volunteer work?

THE CLUES

The woman was a seamstress.
The revolutionaries spoke English.
The woman's volunteer work led to a new symbol for a new people.
The woman lived in the 18th century.
The woman's message was communicated with blue and red dye on a white background.

WHO

CASE 67

THE CASE
Stevie weighed about 100 pounds and stood about 5 feet tall. He didn't speak English and could not see. He wasn't able to walk, but he could run. He was spotted last January in Ely, Minnesota, but disappeared a few days later, never to be seen again.

THE MYSTERY
Who was Stevie and why did he disappear?

THE CLUES
Stevie often made people smile.
Stevie smoked a pipe and never said a word.
Stevie was pleasingly plump.
Stevie perished in the snow.
Stevie wasn't reserved, but some people thought he had a frosty side.

CASE 68

THE CASE
In the dark of night, a daring woman performed feats that few in their right mind would consider. Over many years, she put herself and others in harm's way with her hair-raising adventures, but in the end she escaped unscathed. After meeting her, people were never the same again.

THE MYSTERY
Who was this person and what is she famous for?

THE CLUES
People think of the woman as a great American heroine.
What she eventually did for other people, she first did for her family.
In her eyes, all people were equal.
She helped countless people make a safe passage.
The "railroad" was her mode of transportation.

WHO

41

CASE 69

THE CASE

As Vera idly watches, a well-dressed man speaks to her fluently and rapidly about pressing social issues. Eventually, Vera tires of his conversation. With a slight movement of her hand, she dismisses him and he vanishes into thin air.

THE MYSTERY

Who is the man and what did Vera do to dismiss him?

THE CLUES

Vera has no magical powers.
Vera can speak to the man, but he can't hear her.
The man is seated, but Vera can't see his legs.
Every day the man informs people about important events.
Vera sits in her living room, but the man never comes to her home.

CASE 70

THE CASE

During the light of day, a man trespasses on personal property, taking things that do not belong to him. If no one is home, the man may occasionally go inside and leave hidden messages that can implicate but not indict him.

THE MYSTERY

Who is he and why doesn't he get arrested?

THE CLUES

People anxiously await this man's arrival.
Dogs are not known to be his best friend.
What he takes often travels by air.
He has vowed that weather will not deter his mission.
He wears a blue uniform.

WHAT

CASE 71

THE CASE

A widow gives birth to a son with a slight deformity. Many in her community cruelly taunt and torment the son. When the widow tries to defend him, she is imprisoned. However, as the son grows older, he discovers his deformity has given him an unusual ability that leads to fame and fortune.

THE MYSTERY

What is the son's deformity and what special ability does he have?

THE CLUES

The widow is an entertainer and performer.
The son does not discover his unusual ability until he gets drunk.
A magic feather gives the son confidence in himself.
The widow's husband was named Jumbo.
Mother and son are both Disney characters.

CASE 72

THE CASE

Megan is locked in a windowless room with several dozen other people. She faces a battery of tests for nearly three hours. Megan is under intense pressure and every answer will be closely scrutinized. Her future depends on her ability to answer correctly.

THE MYSTERY

What is Megan doing, and where is she?

THE CLUES

Megan knows that her future will be affected by the test.
Megan had to show a picture ID.
Megan has been coming to this place daily for the last three years.
Megan is only 17 years old.
Megan has several number #2 pencils with her—and is taking a standardized test.

WHAT

CASE 73

THE CASE

A huge storm gathers over the desert one January, threatening everything in its path. Thousands die and many more are injured. The storm passes, but the sky remains darkened by big black clouds.

THE MYSTERY

What two countries were most affected by the storm and what year did it hit?

THE CLUES

The countries have a hot climate and are rich in natural resources.
The storm did not bring rain or wind.
The United States government helped create the storm.
The countries are in the Middle East.
The storm took place in the 1990s.

CASE 74

THE CASE

A man prepares for a dangerous mission at work by putting on a constricting uniform. Halfway through the mission, he senses danger and immediately presses a button. He escapes that threat, but moments later is found 100 feet away unconscious. He later dies.

THE MYSTERY

What was the man's occupation and what was the cause of death?

THE CLUES

The man was conducting scientific research.
The man's uniform came with special equipment.
When the man was found, he was soaking wet.
The man boarded a boat before embarking on his mission.
The man did not die from drowning.

WHAT

CASE 75

THE CASE

Dr. Griffith is a successful surgeon. One day, a car hits his son, badly injuring him. Dr. Griffith rushes him to the emergency room; but, upon seeing the attending surgeon, Dr. Griffith realizes it's impossible for the surgeon to operate on his son.

THE MYSTERY

What is the name of the attending surgeon and why couldn't the surgeon operate?

THE CLUES

Dr. Griffith knows the attending surgeon well.
The attending surgeon is very skilled.
The attending surgeon had not been drinking and was in no way incapacitated.
No one would expect the surgeon to operate under these conditions.
The attending surgeon knew Dr. Griffith's son intimately.

CASE 76

THE CASE

A steady stream of people enter Butch's place of business and remove its treasured belongings. The people do not pay for what they take. Butch allows them to take as much as they can carry, as long as they keep it quiet.

THE MYSTERY

What type of business employs Butch and what are the people taking?

THE CLUES

Butch makes sure his shelves are always stocked with merchandise.
Butch does more lending than selling.
The city government own and runs Butch's place of business.
Sometimes Butch makes people pay when they bring the belongings back.
Butch sometimes thinks of his customers as "worms."

WHAT

CASE 77

THE CASE

A single man is found dead, face down in the snow, far from his home. There are no tracks around him and it has not snowed in several weeks. Hundreds of people witnessed his death, but only he could have prevented it.

THE MYSTERY

What was the man doing just before his death and how did he die?

THE CLUES

It was windy and cold when the man died.
The man paid to be where he was and was dressed warmly.
The man was not wearing shoes.
The man was engaged in a recreational activity.
The man fell to his death.

CASE 78

THE CASE

Stan walks into a large room wearing his robe. When people see him, they stop talking and look up. After a while, Stan walks away and doesn't reappear for around a week. The people all leave quietly. Some leave Stan money.

THE MYSTERY

What is Stan's profession and where does he work?

THE CLUES

Stan is not homeless or crazy.
People look up to Stan.
Stan likes to serve, but he doesn't play tennis.
Stan always works on Sunday.
Stan's not a family man, but he is a man for families.

WHAT

CASE 79

THE CASE

A fleet of U.S. Naval vessels is heading due north into frigid Arctic waters when it comes under heavy enemy attack. One member of the flotilla sinks to the bottom and disappears from enemy radar screens. Although the captain and the entire crew went down with the ship, the rest of the fleet does not stop to look for survivors.

THE MYSTERY

What type of ship sank to the bottom and how many crew members were killed?

THE CLUES

The crew couldn't survive for long in the cold Arctic waters.
No crew member was found in the water.
The crew was prepared for what happened.
The ship went hundreds of feet below the surface.
The ship had sunk before.

CASE 80

THE CASE

Thousands of people attend a professional sporting event. During the event, a person drives around in a large vehicle for nearly a quarter of an hour. The driver does not count the number of laps completed and doesn't appear to be competing in any way. The spectators often appear disinterested and don't bother to cheer when the driver finishes.

THE MYSTERY

What is the vehicle's purpose and what is the event?

THE CLUES

The event takes place indoors.
The vehicle is not part of the event.
The event has 12 active contestants.
The event is more popular in Canada than in Nevada.
The vehicle is not Italian, but its name is Zamboni®.

WHAT

CASE 81

THE CASE

Two weeks after a heavy rain, Nancy walks into the forest with her trusty pooch. Together, they investigate numerous pine and fir trees. In a small pit dug by a rodent, Nancy finally finds the hidden treasure she's after.

THE MYSTERY

What is Nancy looking for and who might want it?

THE CLUES

The item can cost up to $1,000 dollars per pound.
Most often, the item is black in color.
In some European countries, people who collect this item are tested and licensed by the state.
The hidden treasure is edible.
Pigs and dogs are used to sniff the item out.

CASE 82

THE CASE

Some years ago, a man left his job to travel around the world with a famous group. The group evaluated the man's credentials and told him he could not join it. The man was elated.

THE MYSTERY

What was the group's name and in what year did the man try to join?

THE CLUES

The man was an American in his early 20s.
The group was planning a trip to Southeast Asia.
The year was one of great turmoil and the group is a source of major controversy.
The year was in the 1960s.
Uncle Sam made the man attempt to join.

WHAT

CASE 83

THE CASE

The young son of a single mother leaves his home to trespass on his neighbor's property. While there, he steals from the neighbor and takes off all his clothes before running back home. Although he is seen and chased, he is not caught and no charges are pressed.

THE MYSTERY

What is the son's name and whose property does he steal?

THE CLUES

The thief has three sisters.
His father was killed by the same neighbor.
He wears only a blue jacket and clogs.
He is a famous literary character.
He has distinctive ears.

CASE 84

THE CASE

A young girl is abandoned by her family. She befriends a group of social outcasts and joins their gang. After learning of the girl's whereabouts, her family finds her and poisons her. The girl slips into a coma, but does not die.

THE MYSTERY

What is the girl's nickname and how does she survive the poisoning?

THE CLUES

The girl is poisoned by someone she thinks is a stranger.
The gang is powerless to help the girl, but keeps watch over her body.
The girl doesn't get along with her stepmother.
The gang has seven male members.
The girl is from a fairy tale and is awakened by a handsome stranger.

WHAT

CASE 85

THE CASE

Wilma is working diligently in a lab when she gets a tremendous urge for a cigarette. There aren't any "No Smoking" signs posted, and the chemicals she is working with pose no real fire hazard. As soon as Wilma strikes a match, her boss fires her for destroying his work.

THE MYSTERY

In what kind of lab did Wilma work and what is her ex-boss' profession?

THE CLUES

Wilma is completing a specialized task.
Wilma sometimes wears gloves.
The destroyed work cannot be replaced.
Wilma's lab deals more with paper samples than blood samples.
Wilma's former boss is involved in the arts and has a trained eye.

CASE 86

THE CASE

Kim travels all over the world for free without ever buying a plane ticket or paying for lodging. She travels quickly—in some cases she visits three different continents in a single week. She works in every country that she visits, but only gets paid in one.

THE MYSTERY

What is the woman's occupation and what type of company does she work for?

THE CLUES

The company requires its employees to wear uniforms.
Kim is not an employee of any government.
Kim's job requires training and skills.
Kim is usually in charge when she is at work.
Kim has really taken off—and landed—in her career.

WHAT

CASE 87

THE CASE

A deafening sound cracks through the air on a warm summer's day. People emerge from their homes to see about the racket, only to hear the noise again. Suddenly and without warning, several huge objects come charging into view.

THE MYSTERY

What are these objects and where can they be found?

THE CLUES

The objects are associated with technology.
They aim to dazzle onlookers.
It's not unusual to see the huge objects roll, dive and spin.
They have been an institution of the U.S. Navy since 1946.
The sound barrier is not much of a barrier for these tricksters.

CASE 88

THE CASE

Following a shipwreck in the 1960s, a group of survivors safely makes its way to an uninhabited island. The island has no food other than bananas and coconuts. The people make no real effort to farm the lands, yet they never go hungry. The survivors' plight is well known by the American public, but no rescue attempt is made.

THE MYSTERY

What is the name of the island and how many people survived the shipwreck?

THE CLUES

The island does not appear on any maps.
The ship was a small charter boat.
All of the people on the ship survive the wreck.
The boat had two crew members and only a handful of passengers.
You can see the island from your living room.

WHAT

CASE 89

THE CASE
During the invention of the printing press, a man publishes a book that many people already own. The book becomes an instant bestseller.

THE MYSTERY
What is the title of the book and in what century did the man publish it?

THE CLUES
Most people couldn't read when the book was published.
The book had two main parts.
When the man published it, the book was over 1,000 years old.
The book is still printed today.
The book was printed at the height of the Renaissance.

CASE 90

THE CASE
Jack works with leather and focuses on developing new ways to support people. Jack's work often causes women great pain. While Jack's victims don't know Jack, they sometimes pay large sums of money to experience the results of his professional efforts.

THE MYSTERY
What is Jack's occupation and how does it support people?

THE CLUES
Some of Jack's biggest clients are really in step with fashion.
Jack's creations always have numbers stamped on them.
Jack purposely looks toward the ground when he's walking down the street.
Jack works in leathers, though he doesn't have to wear leather to work.
Jack is a designer, but he doesn't make jeans.

WHAT

CASE 91

THE CASE

An oversized rodent lives more than 60 years. Although his name, voice and appearance change over this time period, he never appears to get any older. Employing the use of special techniques but no genetic engineering, a group of experts believes that the rodent can live forever without showing the ravages of age.

THE MYSTERY

What do the experts do for a living and what do they name the rodent?

THE CLUES

The experts are trained in techniques that preserve the rodent.
The experts do not practice medicine.
The rodent's first and last names start with the same letter.
Many of the experts are artists.
The rodent's original name was Mortimer.

CASE 92

THE CASE

Benjamin carries a book of matches in his pocket. Every night he walks into a room full of people, takes out the book of matches and mesmerizes each person in the crowd. He hears gasps, sighs and then applause, but he can't speak while the audience is reacting.

THE MYSTERY

What is Benjamin's profession and what does he do with those matches?

THE CLUES

It's likely that no one else in the crowd can do what Benjamin can.
Benjamin is an entertainer whose act calls for lots of suspenseful drum rolls.
He wears an elaborate costume when he works.
He is in a profession that has been around for thousands of years.
His act is hot stuff.

CASE 93

THE CASE

A masked man is attacked by a gang of five men who shoot at him, then quickly flee. The masked man survives the attack, but the gang returns again and again until it finally quits. The masked man moves to a new location, but the gang continues to come after him. He moves back to his original spot, hoping in vain for a reprieve. The next night, a different gang attacks him.

THE MYSTERY

What is the masked man's profession and how long does the first set of attacks last?

THE CLUES

The man is protecting his turf.
The man gets shot at a lot—especially during the winter.
The gang does not fire guns.
The man is attacked three times by the same gang in a single night for a total of 60 minutes.
The man is goal-oriented and wears a mask to protect his face.

CASE 94

THE CASE

Maria takes small, painstaking steps every night, often using a stick to help her along. Strangers watch her, but no one ever offers to help. The threat of Maria stumbling causes some people to shield their eyes.

THE MYSTERY

What is Maria's livelihood and where can she be found?

THE CLUES

Maria isn't sick or old.
Flashy outfits make up most of her wardrobe.
Her job requires a fine-tuned physique.
She really looks down on her audience.
Her whole family is in on the act.

CASE 95

THE CASE

An aircraft takes off and moves quickly out of sight. The aircraft doesn't use gas, wind, nuclear or solar power—but it flies farther and faster than any craft before it.

THE MYSTERY

What is the aircraft's name and what is its power source?

THE CLUES

The aircraft is part of a fleet.
The aircraft usually flies for 60 minutes at a time.
The aircraft needs special crystals to fly.
The aircraft uses a fuel based on an element with the chemical symbol "Li."
The crew and its aircraft boldly go where no other has gone before.

CASE 96

THE CASE

A man captures a wild animal and brings it back to civilization. Most days, the man leaves the animal alone and the animal ventures out on his own. The animal often gets into trouble, and the man must intervene to set things right. The man is distinguished from others by his distinctive clothing, which he appears to wear every day.

THE MYSTERY

What color clothing does the man wear and what is the animal's name?

THE CLUES

The man has dark hair.
You can read about the animal in books.
The animal's first name is an adjective.
The man is known by the color of his hat.
The animal likes to monkey around.

WHAT

CASE 97

THE CASE

Thousands of people stand in the middle of a city street and look up into the sky at an enormous wild creature. The creature hovers over the crowd and dives toward a group of schoolchildren standing near a famous department store. A group of men struggles to contain the creature with nets and ropes, hoping desperately to keep it from attacking the crowd.

THE MYSTERY

What is the creature's name and where can it be found?

THE CLUES

The creature is big and yellow.
There are other strange creatures flying in the same area.
The crowd has gathered for a national holiday.
The creature lives on a famous street.
Everyone thinks the creature is full of hot air.

CASE 98

THE CASE

A man dressed in blue has a gun in one hand and a sword in the other. He fights and kills fellow citizens in a region of his country that he's never seen before. Although the country has laws against murder, he is not arrested. The man returns home—and lives the rest of his life with a clear conscience.

THE MYSTERY

What was the man's occupation and in what year did he return home?

THE CLUES

The man was a paid killer.
The man was lucky to survive.
The man was killed in an attempt to save his country.
The man was from the North and was fighting for his country.
The man left home in 1860 and fought for five years before returning home.

WHAT

CASE 99

THE CASE

Each working day, Celeste seems to run in circles to get things done. Instead of becoming frustrated by the repetitive nature of her daily responsibilities, she thrives on them. As she sees it, speed is her friend—and the faster she gets through her paces, the better.

THE MYSTERY

What is Celeste's job and why doesn't she mind it?

THE CLUES

She often gets into scrapes with her co-workers.
To be effective, she sometimes has to put her foot down.
If things get out of control, blood will spill.
Timing is everything in this line of work.
Her professional attire includes a helmet.

CASE 100

THE CASE

The year is 1826. Two men who know each other well are not aware that they will both die today. While they lie near death, their life's work is being commemorated by a nation that is unaware of their conditions.

THE MYSTERY

What profession did the men share and what day did they die?

THE CLUES

The men died of natural causes.
The men were both seen wearing wigs.
The men were both American revolutionaries.
The men were Thomas Jefferson and John Adams.
Their revolution was 50 years old the day they died.

WHAT

CASE 101

THE CASE

A man goes to a supermarket and buys three different products. He pays cash at the register and walks away a happy customer, realizing that he's just made a financial contribution to his favorite cause.

THE MYSTERY

What are the three products and what brand is each?

THE CLUES

All three items are edible.
The product maker is well known.
The first item is made from oil; the second is made from corn.
The man picks up the last item in the pasta isle.
The product maker is an actor who donates a portion of his proceeds to charity.

CASE 102

THE CASE

Michelle slowly slides her fingers against the silver blades in her hand to check their sharpness. Next, she looks in the mirror to see how she looks. Finally, she enters an area where a group of solemn people from around the world holds her in judgment. Michelle has not committed a crime, nor has she entered a courtroom, yet the group's judgment may affect both her and her country.

THE MYSTERY

What is Michelle doing and why is she doing it?

THE CLUES

Michelle neither walks nor talks in front of the group.
Michelle realizes this could be her golden opportunity.
The climate is icy, yet Michelle wears very little.
Michelle takes her cues from the music.
Michelle is one of several women being judged.

WHAT

CASE 103

THE CASE

Danielle coordinates the preparation of five, sometimes seven, highly elaborate meals a day. She never gets to eat any of these meals, even though she works so hard to get every ingredient just right. And what's more, Danielle will be the first to admit that she is actually not a very good cook.

THE MYSTERY

What is Danielle making and why doesn't anyone eat her meals?

THE CLUES

Danielle fell into this job by chance; she used to be an interior decorator.
Danielle works with a small army of assistants and collaborators to get her job done.
Danielle is not a chef.
She's always been more concerned about the look of a dish rather than its taste.
Danielle works with a photographer.

CASE 104

THE CASE

A woman is sitting outdoors and is strapped tightly into a seat. She listens nervously to a tall, well-armed man who gives her detailed instructions. After hearing what the man has to say and seeing his gun, the woman promises to follow his instructions carefully. The man lets her go.

THE MYSTERY

What does the man tell the woman to do and what type of gun persuaded her?

THE CLUES

The man carries one gun and has another in his car.
The woman knows she's in trouble, but doesn't fear for her life.
The man did not point either gun at the woman while he spoke.
The woman is sitting in her car on the side of the Pacific Coast Highway.
The man is a cop and pulled the woman over for speeding, but does not give her a ticket.

WHAT

CASE 105

THE CASE

Furious with her black cat, Angela attempts to shoot it. Instead, she hits and kills her elderly father, while the cat flees. To hide her crime, Angela drags her father's body into the cellar and walls up the corpse. Alerted by worried neighbors, the police investigate the cellar and, by listening carefully, quickly discover the body, along with something else quite unexpected.

THE MYSTERY

What did the police hear and what else did they find?

THE CLUES

Being dead, Angela's father was unable to make any sound.
Angela's father was not wearing anything that could make noise.
Angela was unable to see clearly in the cellar while walling up her father's body.
A similar situation took place in one of Edgar Allan Poe's stories.
Angela was shocked by what the police found.

CASE 106

THE CASE

Against the recommendations of her friends and family, an elderly woman begins an unusual diet. Her menu includes a wide variety of foods, but ultimately she eats something that kills her.

THE MYSTERY

What was the first item of the diet and what was the last?

THE CLUES

The woman is probably not real.
The woman made pet owners in her neighborhood very nervous.
By the time she ate the last item, her death was expected.
No one knows why she ate the first item.
The woman went hoarse after swallowing the last item.

WHAT

CASE 107

THE CASE

It's a holiday. Moss hops into his car and begins to drive. He drives for hours in one direction and covers hundreds of miles. When Moss stops the car and gets out, he's in the same place that he started.

THE MYSTERY

In what state and in what month did Moss drive?

THE CLUES

Moss drives a lot and has never had a speeding ticket.
Moss drove in this state last year at the same time.
Moss is in the midwest.
Moss drove during spring.
Moss is a professional and drives more than 100 miles per hour without getting pulled over.

CASE 108

THE CASE

A man puts on makeup and a strange outfit as he prepares for work. What he does for a living makes some people laugh, but his main audience just wants to kill him. Though he always wears loud obnoxious clothes, he really only wants one individual's attention.

THE MYSTERY

What does the man do for a living and whose attention does he want?

THE CLUES

He has an elaborate performance but he's not an actor.
He works in a ring, but it's not one of three.
He works with animals, but they're not trained to do tricks.
He doesn't work in Hollywood, but he still deals with a lot of bull.
He looks like a joker, but his job is very serious.

WHAT

CASE 109

THE CASE

In 1947, a man breaks something in California that cannot be repaired. He continues to break the thing on a regular basis, as do others. The world finds out what he has done, but takes no action against him.

THE MYSTERY

What did the man break and what type of machine did he use to break it?

THE CLUES

The type of machine had been around for more than 40 years when the break occurred.
The man was a captain in the Air Force.
The man passed an important barrier.
The break caused a loud explosion.
The machine traveled at a speed of 670 miles per hour.

CASE 110

THE CASE

Sam has lived in the United States all of his life. He likes the military, but doesn't like wars. He works for the government, but isn't in politics. Everyone feels like they are related to him, but no one has actually ever met him.

THE MYSTERY

What is Sam's name and what is his government job?

THE CLUES

He is extraordinarily patriotic and is a spokesperson for military recruiting.
He began his work during World War I and has been working ever since.
He has white hair and a beard, and always wears a hat.
Sam is not a real person.
Sam's favorite colors are red, white and blue.

WHAT

CASE 111

THE CASE

"Oh no! " cried the crowd. It was a cold February evening in the early 21st century and thousands of people had gathered in a remote mountain town. Millions were watching on television as the velocity of the participant increased. Like Humpty Dumpty, there was a great fall and then the hero emerged from the ground with a valuable piece of silver. "Oh no!" they cried again.

THE MYSTERY

What is the crowd doing and where are they gathered?

THE CLUES

The event was part of a worldwide gathering.
The participant was representing a nation.
The year was 2002.
The crowd was gathered west of the Rockies.
The participant was speed skating.

CASE 112

THE CASE

A man bets on a horse. The horse does not win a race, yet the man wins the bet. The man proves he won the bet with a process that leads to a new invention.

THE MYSTERY

What century did the bet take place and what did the invention lead to?

THE CLUES

The bet was not based upon speed.
Leland Stanford won the bet.
The bet was that all of a horse's hooves are off the ground at the same time.
Stanford used photographs of the horse in motion to prove he was right.
Stanford put the photos together and flipped through them quickly, in order.

WHAT

CASE 113

THE CASE

Jay asks Brooke for her address to send her a letter. Brooke checks the mail everyday, but the letter never comes. She later finds out that Jay was involved in a crash and could not get the letter to her. Jay is not injured and there is no damage to his car.

THE MYSTERY

What happened to Jay and whose fault was it?

THE CLUES

Brooke received all of her other mail.
Jay's Outlook is not a good one.
Jay called someone in the yellow pages to fix his problem.
Jay's work was affected by the crash.
Jay was not in his car when the crash took place.

CASE 114

THE CASE

Jason feels perfectly fit. He has no symptoms of any disease and feels no pain. After a brief exam with a doctor, Jason is told that he needs surgery. Jason has the operation and goes home bleeding profusely and in excruciating pain. The doctor declares the operation a success and tells Jason to go to work as soon as possible.

THE MYSTERY

What kind of degree does the doctor have and what did the surgery accomplish?

THE CLUES

Jason won't be bothered by this problem again.
The doctor is not an MD.
The surgery is often performed on people under 30.
Jason lost four body parts during the surgery.
Surprisingly, Jason was just as smart after the operation.

WHAT

CASE 115

THE CASE

Sara must be extremely careful when entering and leaving her office building each day because it can be very dangerous. Once at work, she sits in the same spot and stares out of her office window. She does not change direction but change is a big part of her job.

THE MYSTERY

What is Sara's job and who are her clients?

THE CLUES

Sara works alone in her office.
The view from her window changes frequently.
At times she may be slow, but others are constantly speeding around her.
She has a lot of money in her possession, but does not spend it.
She often tells people where to go.

CASE 116

THE CASE

A young woman is found dead with a large lump on the front right side of her skull. Detective Cracraft brings in nine suspects for questioning, all of whose fingerprints appear on the bloody murder weapon. He asks each suspect to fill out a number of documents. Detective Cracraft identifies the prime suspect before they complete filling out the paperwork.

THE MYSTERY

What is the murder weapon and what did Detective Cracraft notice?

THE CLUES

The suspects are men who know each other well.
The weapon is very popular in the U.S.
There were splinters in the dead girl's head.
All nine suspects used the weapon.
The suspects are all in uniform and work as a team.

WHAT

CASE 117

THE CASE
A well-known and oft-feared group of people systematically takes money from innocent men, women and children throughout the U.S. Similar groups in other countries operate in the same organized fashion. Despite repeated public protest, the group continues its operations unabated to this day—with overt and covert help from the U.S. government.

THE MYSTERY
What is the group's name and in what century did it first appear in the U.S.?

THE CLUES
The group has its own code that governs its operations.
Congress passed laws specifically designed to keep the group in check.
The group takes more money now than it did when it was founded.
The group is almost as old as the U.S.
The group's annual activity peaks around April.

CASE 118

THE CASE
Rob wakes up in the middle of the night after hearing a loud noise. He quickly puts on his shoes and runs outside where he finds several familiar faces. They all stand facing the building, but don't say a word. They fear disaster, but are told to go back inside after a brief uneventful period.

THE MYSTERY
What sound did these people hear and what are they waiting for?

THE CLUES
They have all done this many times before throughout their lives.
Many were taught to do this in school.
All of them heard the same noise.
They are all neighbors.
The sound is meant to save the residents' lives.

WHAT

CASE 119

THE CASE

Many years ago in the darkness of a blustery and cold mid-western evening, a family decides to make its way to California. Sunshine and beaches await them, but first they have to get there. They plan their route, pack their bags and start the trip to L.A., every minute thankful for the one thing that's making this trip easier and less time consuming.

THE MYSTERY

What helped them make it to California quickly and does it still exist?

THE CLUES

It was once the major east-west artery.
Driving it could be considered an American Odyssey.
Nat King Cole sang about it.
You can get your kicks on it.
Its name includes double digits.

CASE 120

THE CASE

Chris has just finished 12 hours of work. He knows that he will not earn any money for his day of work; in fact, the place where he works has required him to pay them $10,000 for the past 12 hours. Chris is tired, but excited to return to his place of work tomorrow. On his way home, Chris sees the Empire State Building and the Eiffel Tower.

MYSTERY

What is Chris's occupation and where does he live?

THE CLUES

Chris does not work every day.
Chris cannot work alone.
Chris' work requires luck and skill.
Sometimes Chris' work is televised.
Chris works in the state of Nevada.

WHAT

CASE 121

THE CASE

Each day, Tom goes to work early in the morning. Once at work, he dons a little white outfit and then enters a very cold chamber. Throughout the day, he continues to enter and retreat from the cold chamber, each time returning to his workstation with a heavy package. Tom deals with cows, pigs, chicken and fish, but doesn't live on a farm or near a river.

THE MYSTERY

What is Tom's job and where does he work?

THE CLUES

Tom is obsessive about keeping his work area clean.
Tom hates to create waste.
The animals Tom deals with don't make a sound.
Tom sees his fair share of blood.
Tom's uniform includes an apron.

CASE 122

THE CASE

A pane of glass separates an unknown man and a famous woman. The man stares at the woman for nearly three hours. Rather than get annoyed, the woman simply smiles back at him.

THE MYSTERY

What name is the woman commonly known by and what city is the man visiting?

THE CLUES

The woman has black hair and dark eyes.
The man is in Western Europe's largest country.
Rumor has it that the woman looks like the second wife of Francesco.
The woman is not alive.
The man is in France looking at a painting.

WHAT

CASE 123

THE CASE

Each day on the way to work, Kristen and hundreds of other people are controlled by a force that has no arms or legs. While it has no mouth, it can cause Kristen and others to freeze in their tracks. Cars, buses and taxis all fear this incredible heartless enemy, but they also know that it saves their lives every day.

THE MYSTERY

What force has such power over people?

THE CLUES

The effect of the force is immediate, but lasts only a short time.
The force's code involves 3 colored lights.
The force can count, but it only counts backwards.
The force can be seen from a distance.
The force wouldn't be needed if there were no cars.

CASE 124

THE CASE

Peter Oatman works for the Police Department, but he doesn't carry a gun. In fact, he doesn't even wear a uniform. Nevertheless, Peter is usually on the scene of the crime quickly and he is credited with solving all sorts of crime.

THE MYSTERY

What is Peter's job?

THE CLUES

Peter is extremely observant.
Peter never arrests anyone.
There are many people with Peter's skills working for the police.
Samples are required to do Peter's job.
Peter works in a lab.

WHAT

CASE 125

THE CASE

An entire town watches a man in a bright uniform save hundreds of lives every day. The hero has a special sign that gives him this life-saving power, but it is not a ring or a symbol on his chest. He is an elderly man with white hair and a slow step, yet he can stop a fast-moving truck with one hand.

THE MYSTERY

What do people call this man and from what kind of symbol does he draw his power?

THE CLUES

He can stop all kinds of vehicles, but he's no good against a speeding bullet.
Most kids know him well, but he's not in the movies or comic books.
He protects all types of people, but most often he's required to help children.
His sign is red and white.
He is most useful during rush hour.

CASE 126

THE CASE

Sherry enters a business establishment with more than $500 in cash and valuables. After less than 3 minutes, she leaves with none of her valuables, but with a single piece of paper. Sherry isn't upset, doesn't call the police and plans to return to the business establishment again.

THE MYSTERY

What were Sherry's valuables and what type of business did she visit?

THE CLUES

Sherry's valuables include a mink stole and her favorite dress.
Sherry expects to retrieve the 'missing' valuables within a week.
The business establishment routinely exchanges a piece of paper for peoples' valuable possessions.
Sherry brought her valuables in not long after she used them.
The business returned the valuables in a better condition than they were delivered.

WHAT

CASE 127

THE CASE

A man secretly goes to see a woman who he's known for many months. Together, they talk intimately and, at one point, he even breaks down and cries. After a while, the woman writes something down on a piece of paper, gives it to him, and tells him he has to leave. With hunched shoulders, he goes out, planning to return as soon as she'll let him.

THE MYSTERY

What is the woman's relationship to the man and what did she write down during their visit?

THE CLUES

She has similar experiences many times each week.
The man stares at the ceiling much of the time they're together.
The woman is a good listener.
The woman is well educated and displays a framed diploma to prove it.
The man expects the woman to help him help himself.

CASE 128

THE CASE

Peter is a misunderstood teenager who has a very dangerous nighttime occupation. He wears a full-body uniform for his graveyard shift and often finds himself falling off of very tall buildings. Often he fights off the attacks of incredibly deranged characters. Peter never gets hurt too badly and appears to win every fight.

THE MYSTERY

What is Peter's last name and what is his nighttime job?

THE CLUES

Peter lives in New York City with his aunt.
Peter works as a photographer for the local paper.
Peter's certainly doesn't have arachnophobia.
Peter's night job has been captured in comics and movies.
Gwen is Peter's girlfriend.

WHAT

CASE 129

THE CASE
Bernadette picks up a very sharp object and holds it in her left hand. She then very carefully selects some binding material. Others observe her behavior and nod approvingly. Smiling, like an assassin, Bernadette then grabs a second very sharp object and commences to stab the binding material. After several hours she stops and calmly packs up her things and leaves, taking both sharp objects with her.

THE MYSTERY
What are the sharp objects and what is the binding material?

THE CLUES
Bernadette is in a class.
The binding material comes in many colors.
Bernadette is not a criminal.
Bernadette learned this activity from her mother.
Bernadette is creating clothing.

CASE 130

THE CASE
A sweaty, out-of-breath individual walks into the offices of an upscale law firm. She saunters right past the reception area to the desk of a top partner. The partner hands her an envelope and then curtly dismisses her. Though she looks out of place here, her special services keep the partner very satisfied.

THE MYSTERY
What is this woman's job and where could she be found?

THE CLUES
The woman carries important, sometimes confidential items.
The woman carries a radio so she can communicate with her office and her clients.
The woman is in excellent physical shape.
Strong leg muscles are a prerequisite for this woman's livelihood.
The woman's preferred mode of transportation has two wheels.

WHAT

CASE 131

THE CASE

Steve hangs out in a bad part of town, and he loves to drink beer. He is often seen gesturing violently with both hands as he talks in a loud voice, even though no one else is nearby. Sometimes he repeats himself three or four times. Although police officers routinely lock up people who drink as much as Steve does and walk around talking to no one, they always leave Steve alone.

THE MYSTERY

What is Steve doing while he gestures with his hands?

THE CLUES

Police officers don't give Steve a second glance; they think he's perfectly normal.
Steve is usually well-dressed.
Steve is not homeless.
Steve likes to use modern technology.
Steve is having a conversation with someone, even though it looks like he's alone.

CASE 132

THE CASE

A group of four comes together and follows a road they believe will lead to enlightenment. The group's leader brings along a trusted companion. The group encounters alien animals, metaphysical phenomena and extreme allergies during their travels.

THE MYSTERY

What is the name of the leader's companion and in what city does the road end?

THE CLUES

All four members of the group sing.
You won't find the city on any map.
There are no signs on the road and it isn't paved.
The city is named after a precious gem and the road is made of brick.
The companion is a four-legged animal.

WHAT

CASE 133

THE CASE

People come from all over the world to view paintings at a well-known location in France. They marvel at the artists' use of color and perspective. Although the paintings are famous, even experts don't know who painted them, or when they were painted.

THE MYSTERY

In what type of "facility" are the paintings housed?

THE CLUES

The paintings have natural subjects.
The paintings are very old.
The paintings are not in a museum.
The paintings were not painted with brushes and paint.
The paintings record everyday events, and celebrate triumphs.

CASE 134

THE CASE

Gavin is wanted by the police for numerous bank robberies, but the police don't know his real name, or what he looks like. Although he's broken into more than a dozen banks and stolen millions of dollars, he has never actually set foot in a bank.

THE MYSTERY

What is the main tool Gavin uses to commit his robberies?

THE CLUES

Gavin does not use weapons.
Gavin always works alone.
It is impossible for bank tellers to identify him, because they have never seen him.
The police don't even bother to review the images captured by the security cameras.
Gavin is a high tech wizard.

WHAT

75

CASE 135

THE CASE

Nick buys a small package from an unknown man. The package's contents are colorful but explosive, and must be protected by a specialized metal lining. Nick tucks the package underneath his coat and delivers it to a young girl. Upon opening it, the little girl is not alarmed—in fact, she is delighted by what she finds.

THE MYSTERY

What does the package contain and why isn't the girl harmed?

THE CLUES

The product is not illegal in the U.S.
The package can easily fit in the man's pocket.
The package is lined with aluminum foil.
The little girl immediately puts the contents in her mouth.
Legend has it that combining the product with Coke® is lethal.

CASE 136

THE CASE

At a meeting of his church choir, a man became flustered and irritated. It seems that he had real trouble keeping his place in the hymnal, and couldn't flip to the proper songs with adequate speed. He went home in a mood and decided he was going to do something about it. Today, choristers and others all over the world use his solution.

THE MYSTERY

What's the name of this product and its inventor?

THE CLUES

The inventor started working on this product in the 1970s.
His colleague at 3M helped him.
The product can now be found on desks and files everywhere.
Office workers are stuck on this product.
The product is often square and yellow.

WHAT

CASE 137

THE CASE

Bob speaks fluent English (and a number of other languages), and works in a fast-food restaurant. He does not have an artificial breathing apparatus, but he lives (and breathes) comfortably at the bottom of the ocean. Each day, he and his friends visit living rooms around the world, without ever leaving the ocean floor.

THE MYSTERY

What is Bob's full name?

THE CLUES

Bob is a real animal.
Bob is a total square.
Bob's best friends are a sea star and a squid.
Bob is quite animated.
Bob knows Nick.

CASE 138

THE CASE

A man at work nervously handles a small metal device. He cautiously pours a flammable fluid into the device to create an intended reaction. It is important that he be very precise in his measuring of the flammable fluid into the device. Most people see the resulting product as a good thing, but for some it may be life threatening.

THE MYSTERY

What is the man's job and what has he created?

THE CLUES

The product is often customized to the specifications of its buyer.
The product must be delivered in a specified container.
The product can have a debilitating effect.
The product cannot be purchased after 2:00 a.m. in California.
The product can be dry even when it is wet.

WHAT

CASE 139

THE CASE
Wild young Erin goes to five parties in rapid succession. She arrives home at 1:30 a.m. and collapses in a heap, exhausted, on her bed. She wakes up exactly 29 minutes later and groggily walks to the bathroom. Four minutes later she returns to bed, and realizes that it is now 3:03 a.m.

THE MYSTERY
What day of the week is it?

THE CLUES
Erin did not pass out in the bathroom.
Erin really was out of bed for only four minutes.
Erin's clocks don't show the correct time.
It's springtime.
If Erin does the same thing in 6 months, it will seem that she returns to bed an hour before she wakes up.

CASE 140

THE CASE
The deadliest animal in the United States roams the streets of a small suburban community. Every year, these animals kill more humans, in various gruesome ways, than any other species. Nonetheless, few humans are frightened of these animals; instead, they admire and even feed them.

THE MYSTERY
What are these animals called and how do they kill humans?

THE CLUES
The animals do not have large claws or fangs.
The animals don't drive cars, but they like the wide-open road.
The animals rarely attack humans.
Many people think these animals are cute.
Some people hunt these animals.

WHERE

CASE 141

THE CASE

A small, defenseless animal stands quietly in the sunshine. Suddenly, it is hoisted up into the air by a rope and pummeled with sticks until its body is mutilated. Although many witness this, the perpetrators are not punished or condemned in any way.

THE MYSTERY

Where did this action take place and who did it?

THE CLUES

The action commemorated a festive occasion and anniversary.
The perpetrators could not see the animal as they hit it.
The animal is unusually colored.
The weight of the animal is light for its size.
The animal is only valuable for what can be found inside it.

CASE 142

THE CASE

Audrey steps into a long, enclosed area. Suddenly and without warning, spherical objects come hurtling at her at great speeds. She could easily escape, but instead chooses to brandish a weapon of sorts and attempt to actually attack the objects. Friends and family stand by and shout encouragement, but do nothing to help her get out of harm's way.

THE MYSTERY

Where is this person and what is she doing?

THE CLUES

Audrey actually paid money to experience this abuse.
Some might call this "practice."
Audrey has been called a real swinger.
She attacks the objects with a long wooden piece of equipment.
Her favorite team is the Yankees.

WHERE

CASE 143

THE CASE

Years ago, two men spent every day and night together. A third man waited for them nearby. Going outside could kill the men, but they went for short walks and drives nonetheless. Now the men lead normal lives and can go outside as often as they like.

THE MYSTERY

Where were the men and what was their profession?

THE CLUES

The men's job required travel.
The men worked for the government and were selected from many applicants.
The men did not travel in a car or boat.
The men made history.
The men's careers really took off in 1969.

CASE 144

THE CASE

David is a native New Yorker. In front of thousands of witnesses, he dies a gruesome death on a busy street. At the time of his death, David is doing the same thing hundreds of other people are doing. Onlookers cheer and wave during David's demise.

THE MYSTERY

What killed David and in what country did he die?

THE CLUES

David did not die in the U.S.
There was no traffic on the street.
David ran for his life—but died anyway.
David died in Europe.
A herd of animals killed David.

WHERE

81

CASE 145

THE CASE

Mr. Blaine lives in Africa and runs a small eating and drinking establishment, which has become a local tourist trap. One night he is asked by a wanted man to protect a valuable possession. Moments later the man is murdered and Mr. Blaine's life falls into turmoil. The police do not arrest Mr. Blaine, despite his guilt in committing numerous crimes.

THE MYSTERY

Where is Mr. Blaine's business and what is it called?

THE CLUES

Mr. Blaine lives in Northern Africa, where most people speak French.
Mr. Blain's story is told in a movie.
World War II is raging during Mr. Blaine's time.
Mr. Blaine named his café after himself.
The valuable possession includes letters of transit to Lisbon.

WHERE

CASE 146

THE CASE

People from around the world attend a series of professional sporting events, even though they know who will win. The players and referees claim that the games are not rigged and the final score does vary—but the outcome is always the same.

THE MYSTERY

Where is the winning team from and what sport do they play?

THE CLUES

Both men and women have played for the winning team.
The sport was invented in America, but is played all around the world.
The team's players often sport clever nicknames.
Wilt "The Stilt" Chamberlain was one of the team's most famous players.
The team hails from the Big Apple, but has been around the globe.

WHERE

WHERE

CASE 147

THE CASE
The ground beneath a group of unsuspecting people gurgles and groans. Steam escapes from a hole nearby and suddenly a violent sound emanates. This is followed by a stupefying, white-hot display of force. Instead of running for their lives, the people step closer and gaze in wonder.

THE MYSTERY
Where are these people and what are they looking at?

THE CLUES
This phenomenon happens when water comes in contact with magma in areas of volcanic activity.
This display can be seen approximately every hour.
It can reach heights of 106 – 184 feet.
This natural attraction was named in 1870 for its consistent performance.
It can be seen in a national park.

CASE 148

THE CASE
A man walks to a place where nothing will happen for several hours. He stands in a city square with thousands of other people—many of whom are speaking foreign languages. The man checks his watch regularly and looks upward in nervous anticipation.

THE MYSTERY
Where is the man and what is he waiting for?

THE CLUES
The man is in the United States.
The man is waiting for something to begin—and to end.
The man is on Broadway, but is not a performer.
The man receives several kisses from strangers.
The man is expecting fireworks, but it's not July.

WHERE

83

CASE 149

THE CASE

A group of people stumbles across a body. After examining the corpse, the group notes that the body is missing internal organs—but maintains the victim died a natural death.

THE MYSTERY

What is the people's occupation and in what country did they find the body?

THE CLUES

The people have no medical training.
Some of the people are doctors.
The country is in northern Africa.
The country is home to King Tut.
The people really dig their job.

CASE 150

THE CASE

A huge outdoor sign is raised to draw attention to new real estate. The sign costs $21,000, but is less than 20 letters long. Although it is only meant to advertise the prime property for a year and a half, it remains in the same location for eight decades.

THE MYSTERY

Where is the sign located and what does it say?

THE CLUES

The property being advertised is in wooded hills overlooking a downtown area.
The sign was erected in 1923.
The sign is over 50 feet tall and each letter is over 30 feet wide.
The sign is built on the side of Mt. Cahuenga.
The sign has become a landmark of the movie-making capital of the world.

WHERE

CASE 151

THE CASE
A man's body is found 1,000 feet below sea level. Drowning is not the cause of death.

THE MYSTERY
Where and how did the man die?

THE CLUES
The man died of natural causes, but many things could have killed him.
The man died face down.
The man died in a U.S. desert.
The sun was out when the man died.
The man died in a California valley known for its killer heat.

CASE 152

THE CASE
George walks into a room and is handed a number. His belongings are taken from him and he is asked to take off his clothes. A uniformed man escorts him to a locked chamber. An hour later, he emerges from the chamber covered in dirt and sweat.

THE MYSTERY
Where is George and what is he doing?

THE CLUES
George's number was attached to a key.
Only a male was allowed to escort George to the chamber.
George goes through this ritual once a month.
George wore a robe after taking off his clothes.
George tipped the uniformed man $10.00.

WHERE

CASE 153

THE CASE

A man with a large collection of knives skillfully dismembers his victims in a precise manner. The police know where the man lives and where he disposes of the dismembered parts, but never question or arrest him.

THE MYSTERY

Where does the man dispose of his victims and what is the man's profession?

THE CLUES

The man could be in any town in the U.S.
The man rarely sees his victims before they die.
The man works indoors and wears white.
The man dumps his victims in a large metal container behind his place of business.
The man really knows his meat.

CASE 154

THE CASE

A group of desperate men takes refuge in a nearby church. The enemy approaches and the men are vastly outnumbered. A standoff ensues that lasts nearly two weeks. When the scuffle is over, all the men from inside the church are defeated and dead, but people think of them as heroes, not lunatics.

THE MYSTERY

Where in the United States can this church be found and what is its name?

THE CLUES

In Spanish, the name of this place means "cottonwood."
It's a well-preserved historic site.
It figured in the battle for one state's independence.
The enemy spoke Spanish.
It can be found in the Lone Star State.

WHERE

CASE 155

THE CASE

Vito leads a group of people into a dark room that's filled with an overwhelming odor. The people are silent the entire time they are in the room. If they speak too often or too loudly, Vito reprimands them.

THE MYSTERY

Where are the people and what is Vito's job?

CLUES

The people often laugh or cry.
All of the people are sitting down.
The people will leave the room after about two hours.
The odor is fresh and buttery!
The people have paid to be in the room.

CASE 156

THE CASE

A travel-worn and slightly grubby woman walks into an establishment. She immediately takes off some of her outerwear – when she does this, the shop workers get down on the ground. After about 30 minutes, she leaves the business but the workers remain crouched near the floor.

THE MYSTERY

Where is this woman and why did she go to the shop?

THE CLUES

The workers are not afraid of her.
They do this kind of thing for every client.
Sitting down low keeps them closer to the object of their labors.
The woman read a magazine while being serviced.
The woman is seeking a more "polished" look.

WHERE

CASE 157

WHERE

THE CASE

A woman immigrates to the United States from France. Although she lives in New York for many years, she never learns to speak English or hold down a job. Nonetheless, she becomes one of America's most famous residents.

THE MYSTERY

Where in New York does this woman live and who is she?

THE CLUES

The woman arrived in New York in June 1885.
The woman is unusually tall and statuesque.
The woman has a great view of the Big Apple from her home.
The woman is the only resident of the island she inhabits.
People come from thousands of miles away just to see the woman.

WHERE

CASE 158

THE CASE

Dorothy is driving outside in an open space. Her speed is over 100 mph. There are people standing all around her, remarking on her fast driving. She isn't concerned that she will hit anyone and no one is concerned about being run over, although some are standing within a few feet of her.

THE MYSTERY

Where is Dorothy and why aren't people worried about being hit?

THE CLUES

If Dorothy were to hit anyone, the impact could kill or seriously injure the person.
Although her driving is fast, Dorothy would say that she's taking her time.
When Dorothy drives she actually ends up walking.
The people watching are not in Dorothy's direct path.
Dorothy is participating in a competition, but she's not at a racetrack.

WHERE

CASE 159

THE CASE

A man enters a sweepstakes one summer and is notified by mail that he has won third prize: a new refrigerator. The man owns his home, but does not have a fridge. Although there are no hidden costs and he needs to keep his family's food cold, the man turns down the prize.

THE MYSTERY

Where does the man live?

THE CLUES

The man's home borders the Pacific.
The man is a fisherman who built his house by himself.
The house is on land and is made from unusual building materials.
The man lives in the largest U.S. state.
The man's home is round.

CASE 160

THE CASE

In a large, well-lit room, thirty people repeatedly attack a small group of scrawny kids. The people wield a large red object, applying as much force as possible. The victims are greatly upset and publicly humiliated by this beating, but they feel pressured into subjecting themselves to the same torment the very next day.

THE MYSTERY

Where is this taking place and why are the kids being hit?

THE CLUES

Almost every person in the U.S. has had a similar experience.
The group circles its victims.
A teacher is present, but does nothing to interfere.
If the object misses the kids, there is usually only a brief reprieve.
The children are laughing, but try hard to avoid the object.

WHERE

CASE 161

THE CASE

A creature has been living in the same waters for decades. It has attacked several tourists and has frightened many locals. Although it always attacks at the exact same place, millions of people visit that very place year after year.

THE MYSTERY

Where is the creature always spotted and what kind of creature is it?

THE CLUES

The creature springs upon people with little warning.
People pay money to watch the creature attack.
The creature lives in Southern California.
There is a movie made about the creature.
The creature is actually just a machine, but it resembles a very big fish.

CASE 162

THE CASE

Ben has a high profile and an easily recognizable face. Ben's home sits near water, but has been attacked many times by land. Security guards protect his home 24 hours a day, while Ben entertains visitors, poses for pictures and goes about his business with no worries.

THE MYSTERY

Where is Ben's home and what service does Ben provide?

THE CLUES

Ben depends on his hands and face.
Ben lives on an island.
Ben's service requires punctuality.
Ben is big in his field.
Ben's city is part of Europe and is the capital of its country.

WHERE

CASE 163

THE CASE

A group of men take care of a large number of horses near the ocean. Every summer, adults come from miles around to watch the horses. The horses run during the day and late at night, stopping only for short breaks. The men never feed the horses, even though the horses are their sole source of income.

THE MYSTERY

Where are the horses kept and what type of horses are they?

THE CLUES

The horses never stray far from their home and always follow the same path.
The horses have endured for many years.
The horses are found on the Eastern Seaboard.
Riding the horses can have its ups and downs.
The horses are kept on a New York island—famous for its hot dogs.

CASE 164

THE CASE

Nina finishes getting dressed and enters a crowded room. Even though Nina is neither a government agent nor a criminal, her every move is monitored by the roomful of people. Some are taking notes while others are photographing her. Nina doesn't smile and doesn't talk to a single person. She isn't frightened, but knows she'll be in trouble if she doesn't leave the room within about two minutes.

THE MYSTERY

Where is Nina and what is her occupation?

THE CLUES

Nina is not the only one in the room being watched.
Nina is getting paid for her participation.
Nina will enter the room again in 15 minutes.
It took Nina two hours to get dressed.
Nina is forced to change her clothes many times.

WHERE

CASE 165

WHERE

THE CASE
Hundreds of people visit Jim every week. The people respect Jim, but tend to walk all over him. Jim offers no objection and never complains about his visitors.

THE MYSTERY
Where does Jim reside and what is his last name?

THE CLUES
Jim is an American.
Jim hasn't moved since 1971.
Jim is best known for his music.
Tragically, Jim's flame burned out at age 27.
Jim is buried in a French cemetery.

WHERE

CASE 166

THE CASE
A man builds a fortified structure to keep out his neighbors, but dies before it's completed. By the time his successors finish the structure, it is so large that it can be seen from outer space.

THE MYSTERY
In what country was the structure built and what is it called?

THE CLUES
The structure took centuries to complete.
Building started in the 3rd century B.C.
The structure takes its name from its country and is part of a dynasty's legacy.
The structure's average height is 25 feet and it is more than 1,500 miles long.
The structure is a popular Chinese tourist destination.

WHERE

CASE 167

THE CASE

A retired man lives on an island in sunny California in the 1940s. He has a great view, which he stares at for many hours every day from his room. He gets free room and board and is surrounded by others of his kind. He lives out his final days on the island surrounded by very valuable real estate, but feels trapped and burdened nonetheless.

THE MYSTERY

Where does the man spend his final days and why does he feel trapped?

THE CLUES

A lighthouse stands on the island.
The island is now deserted.
The island is near a big city in a famous bay.
The man is no choirboy.
The man has committed a felony.

CASE 168

THE CASE

After years of bloody war on a scale greater than anything in recorded history, one side unveils a secret weapon—and uses it. Many lives are lost and the other side quickly surrenders.

THE MYSTERY

Where was the weapon unleashed and what was the weapon?

THE CLUES

The weapon was unleashed on a major city.
From the outside, the weapon looked harmless.
The weapon was pulled inside the city's walls.
The weapon was a large, four-legged animal made of wood.
A woman named Helen had a lot to do with the conflict.

WHERE

CASE 169

THE CASE

A 12-year-old girl walks into an establishment alone and picks up a magazine to read. She is then cornered, led to the backroom and instructed to sit still and be quiet. Fearing for her safety, she obeys this request, but is attacked with a sharp object anyway. By the end of the ordeal, she feels no pain and actually pays money to a woman before she leaves the place.

THE MYSTERY

Where is the girl and why does she pay the woman?

THE CLUES

The girl has avoided the building in the past.
The woman was expecting the girl.
The girl's mother was with her.
The woman has a lovely smile.
The girl was OK until she opened her mouth.

WHERE

CASE 170

THE CASE

A Danish woman travels to Africa in the middle of summer with a group of friends. One night, the group pitches its tent less than 200 miles from the Equator. The next morning, the woman and her entire party are found frozen to death.

THE MYSTERY

Where did the group pitch their tent and in what country were they camping?

THE CLUES

The country borders the Indian Ocean.
The group wasn't prepared for the cold.
The group was at a high altitude.
The country borders Kenya and is home to the Serengeti National Park.
The group was atop Africa's highest mountain

WHERE

CASE 171

THE CASE
A man goes out drinking every night and doesn't come home until the wee hours of the morning. No matter how much he drinks the night before, the man never has a hangover.

THE MYSTERY
Where is the man's home and what is his favorite drink?

THE CLUES
The man is a sucker for a free drink.
The man lives alone in a European castle.
The man gets his drink straight from the source.
The man lives in a well-known region of Hungary.
The man always has a quick bite before he has a drink.

CASE 172

THE CASE
Over the years, explorers make their way through an area of unmatched scenic beauty. At first they experience awe, but then they see dollar signs. Exploitation leads to the expulsion of natives; eventually something has to be done or all will be lost. A tall man steps in and changes the course of history for this gorgeous place.

THE MYSTERY
Where is this natural wonder located and who was the man that helped save it?

THE CLUES
Giant sequoia trees are abundant here.
It can be found in a famous mountain range.
It became the first national park in the U.S.
Half Dome and El Capitan are two of this park's most famous sites.
The man who helped save it signed a bill in 1864 that made it an inalienable public trust.

CASE 173

THE CASE

Kai and Trevor sit down to discuss their plans. As soon as Trevor takes a seat, Kai leaps into the air. Trevor tries to get him to return to the discussion, but Kai just can't get himself settled on the ground. However, when Trevor gets up off of his seat, Kai suddenly slams to the ground unharmed.

THE MYSTERY

Where are Kai and Trevor and why did Kai leap into the air?

THE CLUES

Kai is sitting down the entire time.
Both Kai and Trevor are less than 8 years old.
Kai and Trevor face each other while they talk.
Kai went into the air because Trevor sat down.
Trevor weighs much more than Kai.

CASE 174

THE CASE

Christopher, an American, traveled to a foreign country to visit John. John is the leader of this foreign state and is the first national leader that Christopher has ever met. Christopher leaves John after an hour and travels on to Italy to have pasta and a nap. While Christopher is traveling John decides to go to church and pray.

THE MYSTERY

Where did Christopher visit John and what is John's title?

THE CLUES

Christopher didn't have to roam too far.
Christopher must confess he has never been in this place before.
Thousands of visitors make the same journey every day.
Although neither John's grandfather nor father was named John, he is nonetheless the second.
John is a religious leader.

WHERE

CASE 175

THE CASE

A woman is visiting a major city with her husband. As her vehicle crosses a landscaped area, she hears a loud crack and then commotion ensues. Bullets fly and while she isn't injured, the woman goes directly to the hospital. Her life is never the same, nor are the lives of millions of others who witnessed the incident.

THE MYSTERY

Where was the couple visiting and who was the woman's husband?

THE CLUES

The woman's husband worked for the U.S. government.
A U.S. senator in the 1950s was in the car.
The couple was visiting the Lone Star State.
The year was 1963.
The shots fired resulted in a tragic death.

CASE 176

THE CASE

An elderly woman is walking down the sidewalk of a busy city street when she suddenly falls to the ground and dies. The authorities search for her body, but don't find it for nearly five days—even though it was on the sidewalk the entire time.

THE MYSTERY

Where did the woman die and why couldn't her body be found?

THE CLUES

The woman was 80 years old in 1900.
The woman did not die from the fall.
Just before she died, the woman admired a bay in the Pacific Ocean.
The woman was headed down a steep hill.
Something fell on the woman during a natural disaster.

WHERE

CASE 177

THE CASE

A waterside bar and restaurant offers free beer at sunset during the summer. At the end of the summer, the owner reviews his records and realizes that not even one of his many customers took him up on his special offer.

THE MYSTERY

Where in the U.S. does this bar operate and why doesn't the owner ever have to give away any beer?

THE CLUES

The bar is located north of Chicago.
The bar offers this special every summer.
The bar patrons laughed when they read the beer special.
The bar owner was not surprised after viewing the records.
During the winter, it snows a lot.

CASE 178

THE CASE

A group of famous people hangs out together every day—though some have never even met each other. Many people have seen them together, but if asked, no one in the group would acknowledge that they've had a blast together.

THE MYSTERY

Where can the people be seen together and what are the people's last names?

THE CLUES

There are four men in the group.
The men are in the U.S.
People look up to the men—literally.
The men are all American heads of state.
The men can be found in the Black Hills of South Dakota.

WHERE

CASE 179

THE CASE
A woman is accused of a crime, tried in an American court of law, and found guilty. The woman has not killed anyone or committed treason, yet the judge orders the death penalty. Her execution is swift and there is no appeal or public protest.

THE MYSTERY
What crime was the woman convicted of and in what town was she executed?

THE CLUES
18 other people died for the same crime.
The town is on the East Coast of the U.S.
The crime is no longer tried in U.S. courts.
Frank Sinatra crooned about the crime the woman allegedly committed.
The conviction was in Massachusetts in 1692.

CASE 180

THE CASE
Cristina is inspecting a cargo ship. She notices several problematic holes in the vessel's hull, but doesn't make note of them or tell anyone about it. Although other inspectors surround her, none of them speak during the entire process.

THE MYSTERY
Where is the ship located and why don't the inspectors speak to each other?

THE CLUES
The inspectors know each other well and are not arguing.
They need special equipment to conduct this inspection.
Even though Cristina finds rooms filled with water, she's not alarmed.
Throughout the inspection, Cristina's feet don't touch the ground.
Cristina enters the ship without using a ramp or opening any doors.

WHERE

CASE 181

THE CASE

Two third-grade girls chat away on a street corner after school. A middle-aged man weighing about 250 pounds pulls his vehicle up to the corner and signals to the children. They have never seen him before, but they both get into the vehicle. He doesn't tell the children where he is taking them and slowly drives away.

THE MYSTERY

Where is the man taking the girls and what is his profession?

THE CLUES

The girls' teacher warned them about the man.
The man lures over a dozen more children into his vehicle after the girls.
One girl thinks the man is creepy, but the others think he's nice.
The school hired the man.
The man has a special type of license.

CASE 182

THE CASE

Late one evening, a young couple gets into a car. The man presses his foot to the floor and the car accelerates through the darkness until it suddenly plunges hundreds of feet, flips over, and comes to rest. The young couple get out of the car quickly, shaken but unscathed.

THE MYSTERY

Where was the couple and what type of car were they in?

THE CLUES

The couple is on vacation.
The young man is not the driver.
The couple is in Florida and is surrounded by lots of people.
The car is attached to other cars.
Just before getting into the car, the couple saw a mouse.

WHERE

CASE 183

THE CASE
A person witnesses a string of shootings while working in a foreign country during the 1970s, but makes no effort to stop them. After telling others about the incidents, the person wins a prize that rewards "courage and honesty."

THE MYSTERY
Where did the shootings occur and what is the person's occupation?

THE CLUES
The person does not work for the police.
The person needed official permission to do his job.
The country borders the South China Sea.
The person is a paid informer, but is not a spy.
The country was a war zone for many years.

CASE 184

THE CASE
Louis and Casey speak discreetly over the phone exactly one week after they robbed a bank together. They haven't seen each other since. Louis informs his partner that he has stashed the money, but refuses to divulge where it's hidden. Louis knows where Casey's kids live and makes Casey promise not to rat on him. Shortly after he hangs up, Louis is released from a locked room.

THE MYSTERY
Where is Casey and where is Louis?

THE CLUES
The call is not long distance.
Casey isn't upset with Louis.
Louis is not a prison inmate.
Casey and Louis are partners in more than just crime.
While on the phone, the couple can see each other.

WHERE

CASE 185

THE CASE

Julio is an American citizen born in 1956. He has never been out of the country, nor has he entered a single U.S. state.

THE MYSTERY

Where does Julio live and what two states are closest to his home?

THE CLUES

Julio is often surrounded by foreigners.
Julio works and pays taxes to the IRS.
Both states are south of the Mason-Dixon line.
Julio can take public transit to the two states closest to his home.
Julio lives in a capitol city on the U.S. mainland.

CASE 186

THE CASE

Every morning Isabel leaves her apartment alone in the wee hours and goes to sit in a small room by herself. In the room she listens to music and talks out loud for four hours. No one else enters the room, while she is there, but Isabel's sanity isn't questioned and she actually gets paid for this unusual behavior.

THE MYSTERY

Where does Isabel go every night and why is she there?

THE CLUES

The room is occupied 24 hours a day.
She is only one of many people who go into the room every day.
Isabel always stays in the room for exactly four hours.
Isabel isn't talking to herself.
The room is soundproof.

WHERE

CASE 187

THE CASE

On February 9, Joseph celebrates his 30th birthday with friends and family. At noon, he packs up his belongings, boards a plane, and leaves his native land forever. After a five-hour flight, he gets off the plane—and realizes it's no longer his birthday.

THE MYSTERY

Where did Joseph begin his journey and how many days away is his next birthday?

THE CLUES

Joseph does not speak English as a native language.
Joseph reset his watch while en route.
Joseph traveled between two large countries and flew in an easterly direction.
Joseph is officially 29 when he lands and will celebrate his 30th birthday a second time.
Joseph drove past the Kremlin on his way to the airport.

CASE 188

THE CASE

Hughes Bank has just been robbed! Two miles from the bank, Lydia is racing down the highway. She has not committed a crime, but three police cars are hot on her trail. Lydia does not pull over—and continues to speed through traffic with the police following her every move.

THE MYSTERY

Where is Lydia heading and what is her profession?

THE CLUES

Lydia has never been to her destination before.
Lydia knows about the robbery.
Lydia will continue at top speed until she reaches her destination.
Lydia carries a revolver—and won't hesitate to use it.
The police will tail Lydia all the way to her destination.

WHERE

CASE 189

WHERE

THE CASE

Melissa parks her car and enters a large building. She is stopped by a man in uniform and is asked to prove her identity or leave the building. Melissa is taken to a machine and several of her personal possessions are confiscated. She then eats a hot dog and waits patiently in a high security area until she can leave the premises and get on with her plans for the day.

THE MYSTERY

Where was the object taken and what was it?

THE CLUES

Melissa bought the hot dog in the building.
Melissa is concerned about a storm warning.
Melissa waits in the room for over an hour before she is asked to leave.
The room Melissa sits in only has three walls.
One of the items confiscated is a pair of scissors.

WHERE

CASE 190

THE CASE

In 1996, a boat carrying an object of extreme international importance lands in San Francisco. Upon landing, a lone man grabs the object and starts to run. Some miles away, he passes it off to a woman, who continues running in the same direction. The object is carried to its destination, where it remains for some time before starting the process again.

THE MYSTERY

Where was the object taken and what was it?

THE CLUES

The city is in the U.S.
The item is relatively light.
The city is south of New York and east of the Mississippi.
The item has been more or less in motion since it was first created and is instantly recognizable.
The item starts a fire every four years and is an international symbol.

CASE 191

THE CASE
A woman whose husband has just left her lets out an anguished cry and leaps off a tall cliff overlooking the ocean. The woman survives the fall—without even getting wet.

THE MYSTERY
Where did the woman land and how did the woman survive?

THE CLUES
The woman landed on a surface hard enough to kill her.
The woman was not prepared to die, but was prepared to jump.
The woman did not have a parachute.
The woman did not land in the ocean.
The woman glided to the ground.

CASE 192

THE CASE
A boy walks into a room alone and is taken to a seat by an older woman who is a stranger to the boy. He is strapped in and told he will not be able to communicate with his family for some time. He cries and begs to go, but is told to be quiet and sit still. Hours later the boy is freed and is told to leave the room. He doubts that he will ever see the older woman again.

THE MYSTERY
Where is the boy and who is the woman?

THE CLUES
The boy is not being punished.
The woman is just doing her job.
The boy's parents are waiting outside for him when he leaves the room.
The woman wears a uniform.
The boy leaves the room in a different city than when he entered the room.

CASE 193

THE CASE

Since the early 1960s a man has awakened each morning and put on his uniform to go to work. The man has a black beard and likes baseball. He loves island life and is the most recognizable resident of his country. He is known throughout the world.

THE MYSTERY

Where does the man live and what is his name?

THE CLUES

He is often seen in a green military cap.
He was briefly exiled from his country before returning to overthrow its government.
His country and the U.S. have had several conflicts since the 1960s.
He is the leader of his country.
The island is famous for its rum and cigars.

CASE 194

THE CASE

A boy walks into a building and stands in a line. When he gets to the front of the line he discusses his current desires with a uniformed employee of the establishment. He waits 1–2 minutes, pays $1.99 and then departs with a white bag. His expression matches the name of the product he has just purchased.

THE MYSTERY

Where is the boy and what did he purchase?

THE CLUES

The building shares its name with a famous American farmer.
The boy is happy.
The boy received a toy with his purchase.
The boy is not a vegetarian.
The boy associates the place with a guy named Ronald.

WHERE

CASE 195

THE CASE

Georgia's professional life is on the edge. Georgia goes to work in the dark and spends her time feeling hot while she goes about her business. She is constantly being visited by a series of truck drivers who want to touch her buns and chat with her while she works. Georgia never raises her voice and often thanks the men for dropping by.

THE MYSTERY

Where does Georgia work and why does she thank the truck drivers?

THE CLUES

Georgia often offers the truck drivers a creamy surprise.
Georgia's customers start arriving about three hours after Georgia.
Georgia's buns aren't attached to her body.
The truck drivers are delivering important materials for Georgia.
Georgia is hot because she is surrounded by ovens all day.

CASE 196

THE CASE

A woman and her boyfriend get all dressed up and go to a crowded place. They meet up with several of their friends and the man professes his love for her. The setting is peaceful and romantic, but then the boyfriend smashes something with his foot and everyone quickly leaves the premises.

THE MYSTERY

Where does the couple meet with their friends and why does the man smash something?

THE CLUES

After the violence, the two are no longer dating one another.
The boyfriend is not mad or unstable.
They take separate limousines to get there, but the woman and her boyfriend leave together in one.
The boyfriend destroys a glass as part of the event.
All of the observers drink champagne after leaving the premises.

WHERE

107

CASE 197

THE CASE

Leslie is a college student who is notified by her university that she can't attend school in September 2006. Her grades are excellent and she is current on all school fees. Not only is Leslie not welcome but there will be no professors or students at the school until 2007. Leslie is notified that she can attend another school for the rest of the calendar year.

THE MYSTERY

Where does Leslie go to school and why can't she return?

THE CLUES

Although this is an extremely rare event, Leslie is not completely surprised.
The university wants Leslie to return in 2007.
The events that led to the university's decision were not under its control.
Many other institutions in the area were also closed for a number of months.
When the event occurred, Louisiana declared a state of emergency.

CASE 198

THE CASE

Monica watches a group of men standing around below her. She sees one of the men get caught trying to steal from the other, while another just stands there and does nothing. Suddenly, without warning, a crowd of people around her stands up, stretches their legs and begins to sing. Monica quickly joins in.

THE MYSTERY

Where is Monica and what does the crowd sing?

THE CLUES

Monica has been sitting in the same place for two hours.
Monica's husband is sitting next to her.
Monica's husband is wearing a silly-looking hat.
Monica ate a hot dog and a box of Cracker Jacks® an hour earlier.
Monica is wearing sunglasses.

WHERE

CASE 199

THE CASE

A woman, with no medical or psychological training, spends each night talking to strangers who come to visit her. She regularly dispenses mood-altering drugs and listens to the strangers' problems.

THE MYSTERY

Where does the woman work and what is her occupation?

THE CLUES

Some strangers don't want to talk but are still anxious for her attention.
Many strangers want to talk to her at the same time.
The strangers tend to become more talkative the longer they are there.
Many of the strangers return regularly.
The strangers tend to drink, but not because they are thirsty.

CASE 200

THE CASE

Sam spends his days in a small room with very sharp objects, electrical devices and an assortment of liquids. Every 30 minutes, Sam attacks another person, but he never gets arrested. Surprisingly, when Sam physically touches his victims, they never scream and when he cuts them they rarely bleed.

THE MYSTERY

Where does Sam spend his days and why don't the victims complain?

THE CLUES

People actually line up to have Sam attack them.
People talk to Sam while he works.
People return every month or two.
Sam likes to sit when he's not working.
Sam's victims pay Sam for his service.

WHERE

CASE 201

WHERE

THE CASE

A group of adventurers finds itself trapped. There are high, steep walls on either side and they are surrounded by water. The group is traveling at high speeds without jet propulsion or a motor. They are inches away from death, yet they continue to keep moving.

THE MYSTERY

Where is the group and what are they doing?

THE CLUES

The group is in a southwestern state in the United States.
The group is traveling on the water.
The high steep walls define a national landmark.
Many groups have traveled here before and survived.
The group is on the Colorado River.

WHERE

CASE 202

THE CASE

After bidding goodbye to his daughter and granddaughter, an Englishman sets out from his small village on a long journey. Three years later he returns, only to find that his village is empty and has been abandoned for some time. Despite some clues and numerous searches, the fate of the village inhabitants is never discovered.

THE MYSTERY

Where is the village and what is it called?

THE CLUES

The man was English, but he didn't live in England.
When the man left, the village had just been built.
The man could not return earlier due to war between England and Spain.
Sir Walter Raleigh visited the village.
The village is located on the coast of the Atlantic Ocean.

WHERE

CASE 203

THE CASE
After a long night of travel, Pierre found himself in a strange land. He did not recognize any of the words that the people spoke as he wandered through the land. He did see lots of water, lots of shops and a beautiful mermaid.

THE MYSTERY
Where was Pierre?

THE CLUES
Pierre is in Europe
Pierre traveled by train.
Pierre started in France.
The land Pierre ended in was Hans Christian Andersen's home.
The mermaid that Pierre saw is a statue.

CASE 204

THE CASE
A man from the Dominican Republic, weighing more than 100 kilos and measuring more than 74 inches, fits snugly into a box. Then he grabs a stick and hits a spherical object toward a green-colored monster. The monster doesn't seem to notice, but a loud thunder erupts.

THE MYSTERY
Where is the man and what is his name?

THE CLUES
The man is at a sporting event.
The man was called a World Champion in 2004.
The man is a professional athlete in Boston.
The man is more offensive than defensive.
The man is known as Big Papi.

WHERE

CASE 205

THE CASE

A man watches as a dodgy-looking stranger gets into his car and speeds away. The stranger drives around the nearest corner and disappears before the man can say anything. After a momentary panic, the man decides to head to work and will try to retrieve the vehicle later.

THE MYSTERY

Where was the man when his car was taken and when will he try to retrieve it?

THE CLUES

The man loves his car.
The man was running late to work.
The stranger drove the car into a concrete structure.
The man will have to pay money to get his car back, but it is not a bribe.
The man does the same thing five days a week.

CASE 206

THE CASE

"Ooh, look at all of that blood!" screams Eve. Steve looks forward about 30 yards and smiles. This is his kind of night. He doesn't try to help or call for the police. He just sits and smiles along with thousands of others as the massacre continues. The victim is shirtless, with a cut above his eye and a broken nose. The unarmed predator leaves the scene without any interference.

THE MYSTERY

Where are Steve and Eve and why does the predator get to leave?

THE CLUES

Steve and Eve knew what time the massacre would begin.
Everyone witnessing the attack paid money to see it.
Neither the victim nor the attacker are bare handed.
The event was promoted as a sporting event.
A winner was declared and celebrated by all in attendance.

WHERE

CASE 207

THE CASE

A woman stands before a group of people. She begins to flap her arms around wildly, moving her head in outrageous ways. She will do this for at least an hour, often longer. It's possible that she'll cry as she flails about.

THE MYSTERY

Where might this woman be found and what is she doing?

THE CLUES

The people in front of her are seated.
She studied for years to learn how to do this.
Her movements are actually instructions.
She holds a baton.
Everyone else holds an instrument.

CASE 208

THE CASE

Every morning Tricia walks five blocks and enters a government building where she stays for 7 hours. Each day Mr. Smith, a government employee, makes physical contact with Tricia. He never says anything and doesn't know Tricia's name. At day's end, Mr. Smith always smiles as he sees her coming. While never convicted, he is an admitted interdigitator. Tricia isn't frightened by Mr. Smith and doesn't report him to the authorities.

THE MYSTERY

Where does Mr. Smith work and what does he do for a living?

THE CLUES

Tricia is 6 years old.
Mr. Smith works for the public school district.
Mr. Smith works outdoors.
Tricia doesn't know how to cross the street by herself.
Mr. Smith is in the safety business.

113

CASE 209

THE CASE

The water woke Max up when it hit his mouth. He did not know how long he had been asleep. Max was miles from home and he had no idea how he would return home since he didn't have his car keys or any money on him. Dressed only in his boxers, he had no recollection of taking off his clothes, which were nowhere to be found.

THE MYSTERY

Where was Max and what happened to his belongings?

THE CLUES

Max was not crazy or ill.
Max had not been in an accident, but he had been celebrating his 21st birthday.
The water had a salty taste.
Max lived in Hawaii.
The tide had come in and gone out again.

CASE 210

THE CASE

Chuck spends his time going door to door, performing unsavory tasks all day. He likes helping people and doesn't mind when he has to go to the hospital. Some people might treat him badly, but others are quite kind; whatever their disposition, they call on him when the going gets tough.

THE MYSTERY

How does Chuck earn his living and where can he be found?

THE CLUES

Chuck is in a helping profession.
He knows his clients inside and out.
Most of his clients wish they were in better shape.
Emergencies happen everyday in his workplace.
A stethoscope hangs around his neck.

WHY

CASE 211

THE CASE

George, who owns a chemical factory, decides to murder his wife. To hide his crime, he attempts to destroy her body by dissolving it in a vat of concentrated acid. His wife's body and clothing completely disintegrated, but the authorities were nonetheless able to find evidence of her presence in the vat.

THE MYSTERY

Why didn't George's plan work and what evidence did authorities find?

THE CLUES

Although George owns a chemical factory, he doesn't know much about chemistry.
The evidence could be seen by anyone.
No one but George's wife could have left the evidence.
The evidence was small but heavy.
It's ironic that it was a gift from George that revealed his crime.

CASE 212

THE CASE

11 big angry men skip church and walk onto an empty field one February Sunday. All of the men work in Massachusetts, but they have congregated in New Orleans to conquer a western imposter. After less than three hours, they are victorious and host an international celebration.

THE MYSTERY

Why are the men in New Orleans and by what name are they better known?

THE CLUES

The men work together 6 months each year in the Fall.
The men defeated many foes to have the opportunity to challenge the imposter.
The event will be the most-watched event of the year.
The men refer to themselves using a name that refers to the American Revolution.
When the men win they are declared World Champions.

CASE 213

THE CASE

Michael is fleeing a stampeding herd of buffalo when he comes to a wide, deep river. To escape, he must cross it, but there is no bridge and he has no boat or materials to make a boat. He cannot even swim. Nonetheless, he easily gets away.

THE MYSTERY

Why is Michael able to cross the river and why don't the buffalo follow?

THE CLUES

Michael has no special equipment.
The buffalo are excellent swimmers.
Michael is not particularly strong; in fact, he is small and slender.
Though the river is full, Michael does not get wet while crossing it.
The buffalo are large animals, weighing over 1,000 pounds each.

CASE 214

THE CASE

Connie is a huge football fan. She never answers the phone while a game is on, and her friends know not to interrupt her. One Sunday, she sits down with her family to watch her favorite team play its arch rival. Connie's family notices she already seems to know the outcome of the game, and she correctly tells them the final score . . . in advance.

THE MYSTERY

Why did Connie know the score in advance?

THE CLUES

Connie is not a psychic.
The game is not fixed.
Connie knows the final score with absolute certainty.
Connie did not have access to a computer.
The game was played on Sunday morning.

WHY

CASE 215

THE CASE

A woman is sitting at home in an easy chair reading a book when a masked man bursts in and snatches her purse. Although the man carries no weapon and is less than six feet from the woman, she makes no effort to stop him. She reports the crime to the police and provides a description of her purse, but gives no details about the masked man.

THE MYSTERY

Why didn't the woman describe the masked man and what is unusual about the book?

THE CLUES

The woman did not know the man, but she knew he was breaking into her home.
The woman was reading *War and Peace*, by Leo Tolstoy.
The woman speaks only English.
The woman did not see that man.
The woman's hands were busy at the time of the break-in.

WHY

CASE 216

THE CASE

Courtney and Mike sit down to dinner in a nice restaurant that serves their favorite kind of food. They place their orders and enjoy their soup while waiting for the main course. When the waiter brings their meals, they notice that the meat is extremely uncooked but they proceed to have a wonderful meal anyway.

THE MYSTERY

Why didn't Courtney and Mike care that their meat wasn't cooked?

THE CLUES

Their soup contains chopped scallions.
Courtney and Mike count rice as one of their favorite foods.
The restaurant is known for its seafood.
Courtney and Mike like to use chopsticks when they eat.
Their meal was served with soy sauce.

WHY

CASE 217

THE CASE
Mel is a model who is preparing to audition for a lucrative photo shoot. The model who is chosen will pose in the shoot immediately after the audition. The model will have a number of close-ups, so a smooth shave with no cuts is essential. But Mel draws blood while shaving, and ends up with two deep gashes covered by two scabs. Nonetheless, Mel is chosen, and earns the big bucks.

THE MYSTERY
Why was Mel chosen?

THE CLUES
Mel is a well-known model.
Mel has a particular specialty.
Mel is a nickname.
The photographer will not shoot Mel's whole body.
The cuts were on Mel's underarms.

CASE 218

THE CASE
A large creature lives in Brazil. It has no claws, fangs or venom, but is the most dangerous creature in the world. Other animals flee at its approach and, where it goes, death and destruction sometimes follow.

THE MYSTERY
Why is the creature so dangerous and what is this creature called?

THE CLUES
The creature is adaptable and can live in a wide variety of climates.
The creature can run, swim, climb and even fly, but is the best at none of these.
Although the creature is dangerous, it is often terrified of small animals.
The creature excels over all other species in only one way.
Although the creature lives in Brazil, its relatives are found throughout the world.

WHY

CASE 219

THE CASE

Herbie lives at sea level, near the beach. The temperature where he lives can get as high as 95° in the summer. Although it's July and the temperature is at its monthly high, Herbie is quite cold and wears sweaters and gloves.

THE MYSTERY?

Why is Herbie cold?

THE CLUES

Herbie is healthy and has normal blood circulation.
Herbie always wears warm clothing in July.
Everyone around Herbie is wearing warm clothing, too.
To some, Herbie might seem upside down.
Herbie has a particular accent.

CASE 220

THE CASE

A group of women attack an unarmed man, pummeling him mercilessly and attempting to inflict severe damage. When they finish, the man is not injured and the women gather around the man, waiting eagerly for him to speak.

THE MYSTERY

Why did the women attack the man and who is he?

THE CLUES

The women know the man and have attacked him before.
The women do not think that they will actually hurt him.
The man is paid to be attacked.
The man wears a special protective outfit.
The women are students.

WHY

CASE 221

THE CASE
In a small Scottish town, a tiny bundle of joy arrived a few years ago. Although she looked ordinary in every way, she was anything but. Scientists and curiosity-seekers alike took great interest in her birth, and soon people the world over knew her by name.

THE MYSTERY
Why was this birth so important and what kind of creature was born?

THE CLUES
She has no father.
She shattered many myths.
Her existence presents ethical dilemmas.
The way she was created may not work for every animal.
She is an identical copy of an adult mammal.

CASE 222

THE CASE
Free divers stay underwater for as long as they can on a single breath of air. Competitive free divers train for months by lifting weights, running and practicing yoga. The current world record is nearly 9 minutes. Although Barbara has never trained to be a free diver, she routinely stays underwater for days at a time.

THE MYSTERY
Why can Barbara stay underwater for so long?

THE CLUES
Barbara is in good shape, but she is not an exceptional athlete.
Barbara can't hold her breath for much longer than 1 minute.
Barbara does not hold her breath while she's underwater.
Other people are with Barbara while she is underwater.
Barbara is in the Navy, but she's not a frogman (or frogwoman)!

WHY

CASE 223

WHY

THE CASE

While performing one of his daily tasks at the hospital, Dr. Mendelsohn asks a uniformed woman standing next to the table to hand him an item. He knows that she is not a trained medical professional and that there are several qualified nurses sitting idly nearby. When the woman hands him the wrong item, Dr. Mendelsohn takes it anyway and says it will do.

THE MYSTERY

Why does Dr. Mendelsohn go to the untrained woman for help and in what department of the hospital does the doctor perform this task?

THE CLUES

She's worked for the hospital for 15 years, but she's never administered a shot.
She doesn't work for Dr. Mendelsohn, but helps him nearly every day.
Although she has no medical training, she's assisted thousands of patients, physicians and nurses.
Before the doctor leaves, the woman hands him a bill for $8.95.
The doctor sees this woman to have his nutritional needs fulfilled.

WHY

CASE 224

THE CASE

Fred is allergic to most animals and avoids them whenever possible. Nonetheless, he owns a small mouse, with which he spends hours every day. He often holds or strokes his mouse, even though he doesn't love it.

THE MYSTERY

Why isn't Fred allergic to his mouse and where does he keep it?

THE CLUES

Fred has owned several mice in the past.
Fred does not keep his mouse in a cage.
If Fred lost his mouse, he would get another right away.
Fred's mouse does not move unless he pushes it.
Fred's mouse does not eat or drink.

WHY

CASE 225

THE CASE

A drunken man leaves his favorite bar at midnight and starts stumbling toward his home. By the light of a full moon, he decides to take a shortcut. Along the way, he trips, hits his head on a rock and passes out. He never regains consciousness and is dead by morning. Although his footprints are visible, his body is never found.

THE MYSTERY

Why is the man's body never found and how did he die?

THE CLUES

The man did not die of alcohol poisoning.
The fall did not kill the man, but it did knock him unconscious.
The man's body was moved from the spot where he fell, but not by people.
The man lived on the beach in Hawaii.
The man died at high tide.

CASE 226

THE CASE

Bob loves to solve mysteries, and he's quite good at it. In one week, he solves more mysteries than Sherlock Holmes did in his entire (fictional) career. Even though he identifies murderers, solves crimes and locates stolen property, no one is sent to jail. Nonetheless, Bob is thoroughly satisfied and looking forward to solving more mysteries.

THE MYSTERY

Why is Bob so satisfied?

THE CLUES

Bob is not an actor.
Bob does not work for the police department.
Bob solves mysteries on his own time.
Bob pays money for the chance to solve mysteries.
Bob loves to play games and read books.

WHY

CASE 227

THE CASE

Jack Hammer creeps cautiously through a smoldering block of burnt-out buildings, gripping his machine gun tightly. Sirens wail, searchlights search and the sounds of explosions fill the night air. Suddenly, a grenade explodes two feet from Jack and, from his perspective, everything fades to black. Jack is killed instantaneously. A moment later, Jack stands up and dejectedly walks into his kitchen to get a glass of water.

THE MYSTERY

Why could Jack get up after he died?

THE CLUES

Jack knew that he would die long before the grenade exploded.
Jack looked forward to fighting, even though he knew the outcome.
Jack has died many times before.
Despite the violence in this scene, no one was hurt.
Jack was holding something in his hands, but it wasn't a machine gun.

CASE 228

THE CASE

Jill Svoboda is driven from her home in Los Angeles, CA to a government building. She meets an official who travels with her for a time and then directs her back to the building. At the building, Jill is fingerprinted and photographed, even though she has committed no crime. Jill drives home with a smile on her face.

THE MYSTERY

Why was Jill smiling and what agency does the official work for?

THE CLUES

The official works for the state.
This is the first time Jill has done this.
The official spends most of his time on the road.
No one speeds when they are with the official, but the official is not a police officer.
Jill spent months preparing for her visit to the building – and is only 16 years old.

WHY

CASE 229

THE CASE

At night in a quiet neighborhood, mobs of people move through the streets, using threats to extort handouts from the residents. Although they continue their behavior for several hours, no one reports them to the authorities or even complains.

THE MYSTERY

Why are these people moving through the streets and what threat do they make?

THE CLUES

Many of the people are frightening to look at.
The residents knew this would happen ahead of time.
The people are not doing anything illegal.
The handouts are edible.
This is an annual event that takes place every fall.

CASE 230

THE CASE

Zack sits on a stool surrounded by his possessions, many of which are family heirlooms. Strangers come by and take his belongings, some without ever uttering a word to him. He is sad to see many of his possessions disappear, but doesn't complain or try to get his things back.

THE MYSTERY

Why is Zack surrounded by his possessions and why does he let people take them?

THE CLUES

Though this isn't his job, Zack is getting paid for what he's doing.
Zack hopes that nothing will be left at the end of the day.
If any of the items are left, Zack could always put them in his garage.
The people who come by are responding to an ad that Zack placed in the newspaper.
Zack is accepting money for the items.

WHY

CASE 231

THE CASE

Ed Motch closes his eyes and ingests a large amount of a potentially fatal substance. This substance can cause nausea, vomiting, restlessness and seizures. Ed does not need a prescription from a doctor and the substance is not marked as toxic. However, in large enough doses it may result in death. Despite this, Ed ingests some of this substance every day at the same time.

THE MYSTERY

Why doesn't the substance kill Ed and when does he ingest it?

THE CLUES

The substance has no medical benefits for Ed.
If Ed doesn't ingest the substance, he may get headaches.
The substance is popular in Italy, Austria and the United States.
Sometimes the substance is powdered; sometimes it's liquid.
The substance is usually black or brown.

CASE 232

THE CASE

Buzz is sent into a barrage of bombs and gunfire with no protective armor besides a standard issue helmet. He is in constant danger, but he never once raises his gun against the enemy. Instead he shoots several of his own country's soldiers. He later receives a medal for bravery in battle.

THE MYSTERY

Why does Buzz shoot his own countrymen and why does he receive a medal for bravery?

THE CLUES

Buzz has never gone through boot camp.
He is paid to shoot his fellow countrymen.
The soldiers he shot were not injured.
Buzz is not a mercenary but his job takes him from one war to another.
Buzz's work brings the war to his countrymen.

WHY

CASE 233

THE CASE

It's Saturday and Jane is alone working on her computer at one end of a large office. Dick runs into the office at the other end and shouts, "Fire!" Jane keeps on working. Jane continues to work peacefully, ignoring Dick completely. Finally, Dick reaches Jane, taps her on the shoulder and pulls her out of her seat. They run to safety.

THE MYSTERY

Why did Jane ignore Dick's attempts to help her?

THE CLUES

Jane was glad to have Dick's help.
Dick did not know Jane.
Had Jane looked up and seen Dick, she would have known that something was wrong.
Jane did not realize that Dick was there.
Jane has trouble speaking.

CASE 234

THE CASE

Margaret devotes a long time to creating an abstract painting. She carefully considers where to place each brushstroke and which colors to use. Just as she is finishing her artwork, a woman approaches Margaret and sees the painting. The woman is immediately furious and puts Margaret in solitary confinement.

THE MYSTERY

Why is Margaret in solitary confinement and who is the woman who put her there?

THE CLUES

The subject matter of Margaret's painting is not at all offensive.
The woman has been pleased with Margaret's paintings before.
Margaret picked an unusual location for her artwork, but was not breaking the law.
The woman has punished Margaret with this solitary confinement before.
Margaret is five years old and knows the woman well.

WHY

CASE 235

THE CASE

Chip is never allowed to leave his home alone, even though he is middle aged. When he leaves his home, under strict supervision, thousands of people come to watch him. Chip is in excellent health and has no known mental problems. He is well cared for and never complains about his restrictive living arrangements.

THE MYSTERY

Why doesn't Chip complain and what is his profession?

THE CLUES

Chip is a professional, yet earns no money for himself.
Although Chip could survive in the outside world, he would lose his job.
Chip is an athlete who follows his instincts when he competes.
Even when he's out in front, Chip is a follower, not a leader.
Chip loves to go to the races.

CASE 236

THE CASE

Marie and her best friend Rose are having a party. As the hostess, Marie entertains all the guests, but Rose just sits silently and stares at the wall. Marie serves her, but Rose never eats or drinks a thing. Soon Marie gets bored and puts Rose in a small room for the remainder of the evening. Luckily, Rose doesn't mind this at all.

THE MYSTERY

Why doesn't Rose mind the isolation and what type of party are they attending?

THE CLUES

The two friends are not fighting.
Rose acts this way all the time.
Food and drink are not required to make this party a success.
Rose is kept in a room with others like her, none of whom talk to each other.
Marie is in kindergarten.

CASE 237

THE CASE

Lucy is suffering from a dangerous and possibly fatal disease. Her family decides that she should undergo an operation, but Lucy is not told or consulted. The operation will be done by someone who has never operated on a human being before.

THE MYSTERY

Why isn't Lucy told and who operates on her?

THE CLUES

Lucy is a beloved member of her family.
Although Lucy graduated from school, she has no degree.
Lucy has a license even though she can't drive.
Lucy's family makes all decisions for her.
The person who operates on Lucy has a medical degree but is not a doctor.

CASE 238

THE CASE

In the midst of war, a king captures a queen and is then, in turn, captured. The captor is not in the military, but does hold a specific rank. All three survive to do battle again, and the circumstances are repeated. In fact, each time that they are face to face, there is no way that any other outcome is possible.

THE MYSTERY

Why is no one injured and what rank captures the king?

THE CLUES

The captor does not wear a uniform.
The war is waged by common people and may even involve children.
The king was captured by a rank just above him.
Like the king, the captor is a real card.
No weapons were used in this war.

30 SECOND
MYSTERIES

CASE 239

THE CASE

A woman in Fresno, CA gets on a bus heading east. She has only $10 in her pocket, but dreams of seeing the Empire State Building. After less than 10 hours, the woman gets off the bus and waves goodbye to the other passengers. She gives the man at the counter a dollar and asks him for change. Twenty minutes later the woman looks up at the Empire State Building and smiles.

THE MYSTERY

Why does the woman ask for change and what city is she in?

THE CLUES

The woman is no longer in California.
The weather is pleasant, but the woman chooses to spend most of her time indoors.
The man gave the woman four quarters for a dollar.
The woman spotted Elvis on the way to the Empire State Building.
The woman plans to see the Hoover Dam later in the day.

CASE 240

THE CASE

It's the first day of spring and a group of photographers gather in a garden full of colorful blooms. Despite the beautiful flowers surrounding them, the photographers focus on four Bushes strategically placed on the lawn. The Bushes are not in bloom, have no visible roots and are of various sizes and ages.

THE MYSTERY

Why are the photographers interested in these particular Bushes and what garden are they in?

THE CLUES

The garden is in the United States.
The Bushes come from the same family and species.
The flowers in bloom are roses.
The garden is located at 1600 Pennsylvania Avenue.
The Bushes came from Texas—and have deep roots in politics.

130

CASE 241

THE CASE

George attends a party, where he quickly gulps down a large iced tea before unexpectedly having to rush home. He suffers no ill effects, but other people at the party who drink the iced tea become violently sick. Some even die.

THE MYSTERY

Why did the other people become ill and why didn't George?

THE CLUES

All the iced teas were exactly the same.
None of the iced tea drinkers were allergic to any substances.
George has no special resistance to anything and drank his iced tea in under a minute.
Everyone drank an equal amount of iced tea.
The people were poisoned.

CASE 242

THE CASE

A man is fishing on a small, peaceful lake in a remote area of North America. While enjoying the sunshine, he accidentally falls into the water. The man is a former Olympic swimmer, but he is unable to swim the 50 yards to shore. Although he keeps his head above water and doesn't drown, he dies within 30 minutes.

THE MYSTERY

Why couldn't the man swim to shore and what was the cause of death?

THE CLUES

The man was in top physical condition.
The man was conscious when he fell into the water.
No one heard the man call for help.
The man was wearing a lot of clothes.
Conditions on the lake prevented the man from swimming.

131

CASE 243

THE CASE

Jules is the guest of honor at a party. He downs seven drinks in a three-hour period. Despite warnings from his friends, Jules runs outside, hops into the bright red Ferrari parked in the driveway and drives away. Minutes later, he crashes into a tree and totals the car. The police administer a blood-alcohol test and find no alcohol in Jules' bloodstream.

THE MYSTERY

Why were the test results negative and why did Jules have the accident?

THE CLUES

The accident occurred at night on July 4, 2001.
Jules was not a good driver, but had never received a ticket.
The test results were accurate, but Jules did break the law.
Jules' drink of choice is carbonated and likely to give him a sugar high.
Jules was born on October 4, 1992.

CASE 244

THE CASE

Jim and his family leave their home in San Francisco and drive seven hours, where they find themselves in a world built by foreigners. Although the creators of this world are known for their impressive building materials, this site does not look fit for human habitation. Jim is tired after the long drive, but feels compelled to stay and examine the area for hours.

THE MYSTERY

Why does Jim feel compelled to stay for so long and what is the foreign world called?

THE CLUES

The family drove south.
The family stopped at McDonald®'s in Carlsbad, California and ordered two Happy Meals®.
The family has toyed around with the idea of visiting this world before.
Jim is carrying lots of cash.
Jim's kids love construction toys.

WHY

CASE 245

THE CASE

A woman hugs her children tightly and kisses them goodbye. As she steps out the door, she falls and screams. The children watch in horror as she flails about for close to 20 minutes but do nothing to help her. Within an hour, they are all one big, happy family again and discuss the incident over a late lunch.

THE MYSTERY

Why did the woman fall and why did the children neglect to help her?

THE CLUES

The woman was alarmed by the incident, but wasn't hurt by the fall.
The children couldn't have reached their mom, even if they wanted to.
The woman did not walk out of a house.
The children had a bird's eye view of it all.
The woman fell thousands of feet, but had a soft landing.

CASE 246

WHY

THE CASE

Many people are gathered and separated into two distinctive groups. The people in one group are all wearing matching clothes and the people in the other group are spectators. Everyone will leave once the first group has taken off an article of clothing and thrown it as far as they can.

THE MYSTERY

Why are these people gathered and which article of clothing will be thrown?

THE CLUES

The crowd is full of young and old people alike.
Many of the people are crying.
It's an important day for the people who are all dressed alike.
The crowd is made up mostly of friends and family.
The people dressed alike are wearing robes.

CASE 247

THE CASE

Julia hasn't eaten in more than a month. She is 5'3" and under 100 pounds. She spends most of her time sitting in a corner sleeping. People come to visit her, but she never says anything to them. Sometimes people bring her food, but she's not allowed to have it. The city is aware of what's going on but do nothing to stop it.

THE MYSTERY

Why doesn't Julia eat and where can she be found?

THE CLUES

Julia is not able to leave her home.
Some people visit Julia to take pictures of her beauty.
Many people take one look at Julia and scream in terror.
Julia is very healthy and well cared for.
Julia's caretakers are the only ones allowed to give her food.

CASE 248

THE CASE

Several people learn that someone has been murdered. The people spend hours following the evidence and attempting to solve the crime. Finally, they identify and confront the suspected murderer, but they do not seek the murderer's arrest or even report the crime to the police.

THE MYSTERY

How do they identify the murderer and why don't the people report the crime?

THE CLUES

The murder occurs in a mansion.
The murder weapon is also discovered.
The people investigate by questioning one another.
The murder was committed with a revolver.
The murder took place in the conservatory.

WHY

CASE 249

THE CASE
Sue is an accomplished sculptor. She crafts beautiful pieces that weigh hundreds of pounds and carefully delivers them to her clients. Within 24 hours of delivery, every sculpture disappears. Sue does not seem to be upset by these disappearances.

THE MYSTERY
Why isn't Sue upset and what happens to the sculptures?

THE CLUES
The sculptures haven't been stolen.
Sue must work quickly.
Everyone agrees that Sue's sculptures are cool.
You won't find the sculptures in a museum.
The sculptures are made from a common material, and are heat sensitive.

CASE 250

WHY

THE CASE
It is late on Halloween and Sally enters her home. She searches the house, but her parents and younger brothers are nowhere to be found. As she enters the dark living room, she hears a voice say that he is coming to get her. Sally doesn't call the cops or leave the house and is not frightened or alarmed.

THE MYSTERY
Why isn't Sally afraid of the voice and where is it coming from?

THE CLUES
Sally is 13 years old and is scared of being home alone.
Her parents told her they'd be home when she got back from trick-or-treating with her friends.
The person whose voice Sally hears knows she's alone and knows where she lives.
The voice is coming from a machine.
The rest of her family lost track of time while trick-or-treating.

CASE 251

THE CASE

A man from Chicago deliberately puts on shorts and a tank top, then goes outside in the middle of winter and walks along a lake. The wind is blowing and it's 20° outside, but the man is delighted that he's not bundled up for the winter like the rest of the residents of Chicago.

THE MYSTERY

Why can the man tolerate the weather and what is he doing?

THE CLUES

The man is quite comfortable and, from a physical standpoint, is quite average.
The man's wife is dressed in a similar fashion.
The man is far from his work and home.
The man was recently a passenger on an airplane.
The forecast predicts that the weather will be molto caldo oggi.

CASE 252

THE CASE

Dr. Cooper, a registered surgeon, goes into surgery and immediately passes out. The operation is finished by the time that Dr. Cooper comes to. After a quick physical, he is called upon to perform an operation on a young child. Even though the hospital authorities know that the patient will die if Dr. Cooper passes out again, no other surgeons are present.

THE MYSTERY

Why did Dr. Cooper pass out and why is he trusted to perform the operation on the child?

THE CLUES

Dr. Cooper is an experienced surgeon.
Dr. Cooper's operation was a success.
It did not surprise anyone that Dr. Cooper passed out.
Even after Dr. Cooper passed out, the operation could not have proceeded without him.
Dr. Cooper was not operating when he passed out.

CASE 253

THE CASE

Bob and Ursula are having an intense conversation while Bob is trying to concentrate on driving their two-seater sports car down a winding mountainous road. Bob has a seat belt on, but Ursula does not. Suddenly, a truck swerves and hits their car head on. Their car is totaled, with equal damage on the driver's side and the passenger's side. Bob has two broken legs and a broken pelvis, but Ursula doesn't have a scratch on her body. Ursula calls the police right away, but can't tell them where the accident happened.

THE MYSTERY

Why isn't Ursula injured and why doesn't she know where the accident occurred?

THE CLUES

Ursula was not wearing any special protection.
Ursula was not disoriented by the impact of the crash and was not thrown from the car.
Ursula has a good sense of direction and good vision, but she never saw the other car coming.
Ursula could hear Bob but couldn't see him.
Ursula was not close to the scene of the accident.

CASE 254

THE CASE

An elderly woman goes for a leisurely walk. Two young men in excellent physical condition are directly behind her, sprinting toward her. No matter how fast they run, they do not catch up with the woman.

THE MYSTERY

Why can't the men catch up with the woman and where are all three people?

THE CLUES

The men are running as fast as they can.
The men always stay seven feet behind the woman.
All three people paid money to be where they are.
The men are not moving forward.
All three people are indoors.

CASE 255

THE CASE
A group of uniformed men calmly and methodically enters a house during broad daylight and takes every possession that a family owns. The family does not contact the police, but does find their belongings three days later.

THE MYSTERY
Why weren't the authorities involved and where did the family find their belongings?

THE CLUES
The men are not part of any government agency.
The men are known for taking things.
The family found their belongings in a different city.
The belongings were exactly where the family expected them to be.
The family gave the men money, but it was not a ransom for their belongings.

CASE 256

THE CASE
A lonely man falls in love with a beautiful foreign woman. The woman is a great swimmer, but is afraid to go in the water. The man loves the water, but prefers the woman.

THE MYSTERY
Why is this woman afraid of water and who is she?

THE CLUES
The man gives the woman a new name.
The woman saved the man's life once, a long time ago.
The woman is tall, blonde and beautiful, but sometimes her skin is scaly.
The woman learns the man's language by watching TV.
The man and woman are characters in a movie based on an old fairy tale.

WHY

CASE 257

THE CASE
Toni wanders methodically up and down the same few city blocks each day. She walks with purpose but takes her time. Every once in a while she stops, consults her surroundings and takes something out of her pocket. The folks who live in the neighborhood can't stand the sight of her.

THE MYSTERY
Why don't people like Toni and what is she doing?

THE CLUES
In her pocket is a pad of paper.
She's been berated more than once for doing her job.
Begging her doesn't help.
People run to their cars when they see her.
Lovely Rita is well-known for doing this job.

CASE 258

THE CASE
A man speeds off in his car. After driving for a brief period, he suddenly steers the car off a high cliff, destroying it. There are numerous witnesses to this dangerous act, but no one is upset by it.

THE MYSTERY
Why did the man crash the car and who is he?

THE CLUES
The man was not unhappy or suicidal.
The man has done similar things before.
The man was not injured, and did not expect to be.
While crashing the car, the man is pretending to be someone else.
The man's actions were recorded on camera.

WHY

CASE 259

THE CASE

A family of four is relaxing in their home. Suddenly, a giant prehistoric creature invades their living room. The two children shout when they see the creature and enter a trance-like state. The parents flee the room, leaving the children alone with the creature.

THE MYSTERY

Why do the parents leave the room and what is the creature's official name?

THE CLUES

The creature stands upright on two legs.
The creature can communicate with children.
The parents know that the creature will leave within an hour.
The parents are not afraid of the creature, but are not amused by it either.
The creature is purple and enters homes throughout the U.S. simultaneously.

CASE 260

THE CASE

Jenny is moving into her new apartment. The place is filthy and there are cobwebs everywhere. As she prepares her first meal in the kitchen, she finds a mouse in her box of canned goods. Jenny calmly removes the mouse and continues cooking, not bothering to wash her hands or call the landlord.

THE MYSTERY

Why isn't Jenny worried about the mouse and how did it get into her box of canned food?

THE CLUES

The mouse didn't eat any of Jenny's food.
When Jenny's cat saw the mouse, it didn't pay it any attention.
Jenny brought the mouse over from her previous apartment.
The mouse is clean and free of any diseases.
Jenny packed up her belongings in a rush when moving out of her previous apartment.

CASE 261

THE CASE

"Lucky" Jim is a world-class runner. While the world looks on, Jim wins his most important race, but trips and falls just past the finish line. Jim is quickly rushed away in an ambulance. The next day, a man poisons and kills him. Given Jim's fame, his death was front-page news. Although the authorities know who killed Jim, they make no effort to arrest or charge the killer.

THE MYSTERY

Why wasn't Jim's killer charged with murder and what race did Jim win?

THE CLUES

Jim's killer did not break any laws.
Jim ran after racing a distance of $1\frac{1}{2}$ miles.
Jim broke his leg in the fall.
Jim's killer is a doctor who practices in Belmont, New York.
Jim is less than four years old.

CASE 262

THE CASE

Andy wakes up early one morning and drives to a local school. Once inside he patiently waits. When his turn comes Andy walks into a small curtained room. He then punches away for about 10 minutes. When he finishes Andy feels triumphant, walks to his car and drives away without a scratch on him.

THE MYSTERY

Why did Andy go to the school and what was he punching?

THE CLUES

It was a November morning in 2000.
Andy does not have any children attending the school.
The school was only a temporary place for punching.
The punching involved a piece of paper.
Andy is a U.S. citizen.

CASE 263

WHY

THE CASE

Tami travels extensively and has visited seven countries in the past six months. Throughout her trip, she's stayed in luxurious five-star hotels and has taken advantage of every available amenity from room service to daily spa treatments. The management is well aware that she will skip out without paying, but never confronts her about her clandestine freeloading. In fact, they invite her to come back again soon.

THE MYSTERY

Why is the hotel management so nice to Tami and what is her job?

THE CLUES

Tami always travels alone.
She does not work for any of the hotels in which she was staying.
None of the hotels in which she was staying are owned by the same company.
Tami does not accept bribes.
Tami takes thorough notes that will be published.

CASE 264

THE CASE

With pounding hearts, six women take off running when they hear a gunshot. Without even a second glance at the women, the man with the gun calmly lowers the still-smoking revolver and walks away. He does not fire another shot, but makes no attempt to flee. The entire scene is captured by live TV news cameras, but no arrest is made.

THE MYSTERY

Why did the man shoot and how far away from the man did the women run?

THE CLUES

The man shoots guns on a regular basis.
The man does not know any of the women personally.
The women were expecting to hear a shot.
The women ran as fast as they could without looking back until they reached a barrier.
The man is paid to shoot, but he's never hit anyone.

CASE 265

THE CASE

Alvin is a healthy young man with no major health problems. One day as he's driving to work, something repeatedly happens to his body that causes his heart to stop. Each attack is so violent that he is unable to open his eyes whenever it occurs. When he recovers, he continues driving as if nothing had happened.

THE MYSTERY

What is happening to Alvin and why does he continue to drive in a carefree manner?

THE CLUES

Alvin is only able to keep one hand on the wheel during each attack.
The attacks force Alvin to make a loud, strange noise.
Alvin feels like his brain is coming out of his nose.
Alvin's heart only stops for a second each time he is attacked.
Alvin's car is very dusty.

CASE 266

THE CASE

In addition to pictures of his wife and children, Peter Cannon carries pictures of a number of dead people with him at all times. Peter admires the people, but they are not members of his family. Even though some of the pictures are extremely valuable, Peter often gives them away.

THE MYSTERY

Why does Peter carry the pictures and why does he give them away?

THE CLUES

The people in the pictures are famous and he gives some away every day.
The fewer number of pictures that Peter gives away, the better he feels.
The pictures are wallet-sized and were not taken with a camera.
Peter trades the pictures for things that he wants.
Peter once had a picture of Grover Cleveland; it was his favorite.

CASE 267

THE CASE

Alexandra spends her day making people wince, sometimes scream, in pain. But people seek her out and pay her money to do this work. Sometimes her clients may even bleed a little, but they almost always come back for more.

THE MYSTERY

What is Alexandra's job and why are her clients bleeding?

THE CLUES

Most of Alexandra's clients return to her month after month.
In many U.S. states, she cannot practice her craft without a license.
Alexandra likes to poke around at work.
The tools of her trade can all fit nicely in a small box, not much bigger than her hand.
People come to her with all kinds of ailments, from headaches to terminal illness.

CASE 268

THE CASE

An excited crowd lines the street, waiting impatiently for the main event. They shuffle their feet and gaze about anxiously, arching their necks for a better view. But moments later, before they catch sight of the event they've come to witness, they all quickly scatter. They know there is no real danger, but quickly give up their prized curbside spots and run for cover anyway.

THE MYSTERY

Why has the crowd gathered and what makes them run for cover?

THE CLUES

There are lots of families in the crowd.
What occurred is completely natural.
They are in a city or town.
The sky above them became dark.
The performers – and the on-lookers – probably got wet.

CASE 269

THE CASE

A scuba diver is 1,000 feet below the surface when the oxygen in his tank runs out. The diver doesn't make it to the surface for nearly three hours, yet he doesn't die when his oxygen runs out.

THE MYSTERY

Why didn't the diver die when his oxygen ran out and how did he reach the surface?

THE CLUES

The man was an experienced diver.
The diver didn't know that his oxygen supply had been exhausted.
It was impossible for the diver to die from lack of air.
The diver did not reach the surface under his own power.
The diver died from a heart attack.

CASE 270

THE CASE

Bob is a government employee who spends his entire work day sitting down. His customers pay money and watch him sit. Bob ignores these customers while he looks outside through his office window. If Bob does his job correctly, the customers leave as soon as he is finished.

THE MYSTERY

Why do the customers leave and what is Bob's job?

THE CLUES

The customers keep moving all the time they're with Bob.
Bob works for the city and has a great view of the city.
The customers sit while they are with Bob.
When the customers leave Bob they are on the street.
Bob drives a vehicle.

CASE 271

THE CASE

Jack Jensen is an All-Star baseball player near the end of an illustrious career in which he broke numerous records. He's been a starting player since he broke into the majors, and he's never been pulled for a pinch hitter. In his final game, played at the opponent's stadium, Jensen earns a huge ovation from the crowd as he steps up to the plate for the first time ever.

THE MYSTERY

Why hasn't Jensen hit before and what month is it?

THE CLUES

Jensen was a decent hitter in college and has shown up for batting practice for his entire career.
Jensen's team has lost more games than it won for the past 11 years, but has finally had a winning season.
Jensen handles the ball on every play when he's on the field and his hitting is a sign of his team's success.
Jensen has never played baseball in this month before.
The game is played in St. Louis, Missouri.

CASE 272

THE CASE

At an ancient boarding school, a small girl awakes in the middle of the night in great pain. She's rushed to the hospital, for an emergency operation. Her mother and father don't make it to the hospital, but she doesn't seem to mind. She's comforted by her school friends. Millions of others know her by name.

THE MYSTERY

Why is the little girl so well-known and what is her name?

THE CLUES

When she and her classmates go out, they walk in two straight lines.
She lives in Paris.
The house where she stays is covered with vines.
She loves winter, snow and ice.
She is the title character in books and movies.

WHY

CASE 273

THE CASE

Josh loves mysticism, fun and adventure. Unfortunately, he wakes up one morning feeling heavy and notices his clothes no longer fit. Unable to figure out what's going on, he goes downstairs to greet his mother, who takes one look at him and screams. Dismayed, Josh immediately leaves home with no plans to return. After several weeks of trying to adjust to a new lifestyle, Josh returns home and everything becomes normal again.

THE MYSTERY

Why does Josh's mother scream and where does he go when he runs away?

THE CLUES

Josh's pajama bottoms seem to have shrunk and now go down only to his knees.
Josh doesn't recognize his own face when he looks in the mirror.
Josh vaguely remembers making a wish at a carnival the day before the incident.
Josh falls in love, but it can't last.
Josh runs away to a big bustling city.

CASE 274

THE CASE

Just before closing time, a group of heavily-armed men jump out of a vehicle and cautiously enter a bank. One man stays with the vehicle and keeps the motor running. The group's leader approaches a teller and hands her a note. The teller opens the vault and the men take tens of thousands of dollars. Even after the men are gone, the teller does not trip the alarm.

THE MYSTERY

Why doesn't the teller trip the alarm and what type of vehicle are the men driving?

THE CLUES

The vehicle is designed for quick get-aways.
The teller has seen the men before.
The teller was in on the job, but committed no crime.
The vehicle heads for another bank.
The vehicle is well-marked.

WHY

WHY

CASE 275

THE CASE

A man lives on the top floor of a high-rise apartment building. Every day he takes the elevator down and walks to work. When he returns from work, he often takes the elevator halfway up and then walks up the stairs the rest of the way to his apartment. However, on rainy days, he takes the elevator all the way up.

THE MYSTERY

Why does the man take the stairs part way up when it's not raining, and the elevator all the way up when it is?

THE CLUES

The man doesn't like to ask for help.
The man does not prefer walking to riding the elevator.
The man carries an umbrella on rainy days.
The man was not a popular pick for basketball in gym class.
The man is shorter than his 11-year-old niece.

CASE 276

THE CASE

Mary is a well-known artist. In celebration for her big exhibition, she uses her best brushes, oils and pencils to paint herself. It takes her a long time to perfect her work, but when she steps back to admire what she's done, she is very proud. No one seems to notice these latest efforts during the show, but Mary still feels the night was a big success.

THE MYSTERY

Why doesn't anyone pay attention to Mary's latest work and why doesn't this bother her?

THE CLUES

Whenever someone tells Mary that she looks nice, she changes the topic.
Mary bought her pencils and brushes at the mall.
Mary most often works with clay or chisels.
Mary required a crew of people to carry her work into the gallery.
Mary wanted to look her best for the exhibition.

CASE 277

THE CASE

With painstaking attention to detail, Candy writes down all the lurid, juicy specifics of a crime. She is not a police officer, but she wears a uniform. Candy follows every word spoken with great interest, but she isn't involved with anyone in the trial and has no vested interest in the outcome.

THE MYSTERY

Why does Candy follow the crime and what does she do for a living?

THE CLUES

Candy has followed crimes like this before.
Candy is not a journalist or a law student.
Candy is paid to follow the crime.
Candy works for the court.
Candy is sitting on a bench and is wearing a robe.

CASE 278

THE CASE

Lulu leaves her house and goes into a nearby park. There she begins to eat a large amount of worms, chewing vigorously in order to break up their rubbery bodies. Strangely enough, she suffers no ill effects; in fact, she repeats her action a few days later.

THE MYSTERY

What kind of worms did Lulu eat and why didn't she get sick?

THE CLUES

Lulu is human.
Lulu did not get the worms in the park.
These worms are not found in the dirt.
Lulu's worms are native to Germany.
These worms come in a variety of flavors.

CASE 279

THE CASE

Nina and Maia are making a fortune in real estate. Even though Nina never breaks the law, she is sent to jail. Maia follows the same procedures as Nina with many of the same properties, but she never goes to jail.

THE MYSTERY

Why did Nina go to jail and what is the maximum amount of time she could spend there?

THE CLUES

Nina has been in jail before.
Nina never had a trial before she was instructed to go to jail.
Nina never leaves her home when she goes to jail.
Nina didn't collect any money on her way to jail.
Nina needs a good roll—not parole.

CASE 280

THE CASE

Two sworn enemies take to the seas during wartime, employing their respective naval fleets for battle. With cunning strategy and precise battle plans, each hopes to outwit the other. Even though it's all-out war, each side is sure that none of its recruits will perish during the fighting.

THE MYSTERY

Why aren't the enemies worried about casualties and what is this battle called?

THE CLUES

Gunners await the command on both sides.
Fire will be exchanged one shell at a time.
Neither fleet is on the ocean.
The battle will not be over until one fleet is sunk entirely.
It will take between two and three hits to sink each vessel.

SOLUTIONS

CASE 1 SOLUTION

Harry Potter is the most famous student at Hogwarts.

CASE 2 SOLUTION

The man is Jackson Pollock, famous for his large-scale Abstract Expressionist artwork composed of dripped, spilled and flung paint.

CASE 3 SOLUTION

The man is William Shakespeare; his most famous victims are Romeo and Juliet.

CASE 4 SOLUTION

Buzz Aldrin is an astronaut—and the first person to play golf on the moon.

CASE 5 SOLUTION

The woman is a real estate agent and has entered the house to preview it.

CASE 6 SOLUTION

Martin Luther King, Jr. was assassinated in Memphis in 1968.

CASE 7 SOLUTION

Michelangelo painted the ceiling of the Sistine Chapel.

CASE 8 SOLUTION

The man is Willy Wonka. He lives in a chocolate factory.

CASE 9 SOLUTION

The man is Bill Gates and the organization is Microsoft®.

CASE 10 SOLUTION

The patriot is Yankee Doodle Dandy and the pasta is macaroni.

CASE 11 SOLUTION

Anne Boleyn was the second wife of King Henry VIII.

CASE 12 SOLUTION

The men are garbage men collecting trash.

CASE 13 SOLUTION

The man is Moses and the place is Mount Sinai.

CASE 14 SOLUTION

The man is Santa Claus and he lives at the North Pole.

CASE 15 SOLUTION

The woman is a trapeze artist who misses her catch. She survives the fall because the safety net catches her.

CASE 16 SOLUTION

George Washington used a hatchet to chop down his family's cherry tree.

CASE 17 SOLUTION

The man is the family doctor, who is making a house call. Anthony's wife hasn't been speaking to him because she has laryngitis.

CASE 18 SOLUTION

The man is a police sketch artist named Art.

CASE 19 SOLUTION

It's Bugs Bunny. His favorite catchphrase is, "What's up, Doc?"

CASE 20 SOLUTION

Charles Lindbergh's plane is The Spirit of Saint Louis.

CASE 21 SOLUTION

Laurel was a bay laurel tree. The person sold the tree for firewood.

CASE 22 SOLUTION

The man is a mime who collects money from some of the people who watch his act.

CASE 23 SOLUTION

Christopher Columbus set sail in 1492, hoping to discover a new route to India.

CASE 24 SOLUTION

The stranger is Vickie's date. He is taking her to the prom.

CASE 25 SOLUTION

The presidential family lives in the White House in Washington, D.C.

CASE 26 SOLUTION

The man is the Gingerbread Man who was eaten by a fox.

CASE 27 SOLUTION

The man's name is Clark Kent (or Superman) and there is an "S" on his uniform.

CASE 28 SOLUTION

Samson's hair was the key to his strength.

CASE 29 SOLUTION

Walt Disney built the castle as part of Disneyland®.

CASE 30 SOLUTION

Amelia Earhart was a pilot.

CASE 31 SOLUTION

He is John Grisham; he became a best-selling author.

CASE 32 SOLUTION

The visitors are monkeys in the zoo.

CASE 33 SOLUTION

Parker is one of the Three Little Pigs. The Big Bad Wolf is his enemy.

CASE 34 SOLUTION

The male is a baby and the female is a doctor (obstetrician).

CASE 35 SOLUTION

Paul Revere yelled, "The British are coming!"

CASE 36 SOLUTION

The woman is a professional exterminator. She poisons her victims.

CASE 37 SOLUTION

Jack traded his family's cow for a handful of magic beans.

CASE 38 SOLUTION

The stars are criminals wanted by the police and the FBI. They are featured on America's Most Wanted™.

CASE 39 SOLUTION

Vinnie's wife took out the contract; Vinnie isn't worried because it's a life insurance contract.

CASE 40 SOLUTION

The employees are the Boston Red Sox. They are battling the Green Monster in Fenway Park.

CASE 41 SOLUTION

The boy is Peter Pan. He was looking for his shadow.

CASE 42 SOLUTION

Humpty Dumpty appears in a Mother Goose rhyme.

CASE 43 SOLUTION

Francis Scott Key wrote the "Star Spangled Banner" near Baltimore, Maryland.

CASE 44 SOLUTION

She is Shirley Temple (Black). She endorsed the "Good Ship Lollipop."

CASE 45 SOLUTION

Dr. Jonas Salk invented a vaccine against polio.

CASE 46 SOLUTION

The individual is the Cat in the Hat®. Dr. Seuss (Theodor Geisel) made him famous.

CASE 47 SOLUTION

Bill is a $1 bill of U.S. currency and he is in a cash register.

CASE 48 SOLUTION

The man is Davy Crockett and he is from Tennessee.

CASE 49 SOLUTION

The man is Austin Powers. He's a spy for the British government.

CASE 50 SOLUTION

He is the Man in the Moon, whose face people see when gazing into space.

CASE 51 SOLUTION

The woman is Wonder Woman®. She is from Paradise Island.

CASE 52 SOLUTION

The man is Elvis Presley and the mob has gathered to see him perform.

CASE 53 SOLUTION

He is a plumber who has just unclogged a drain.

CASE 54 SOLUTION

She is Alice and she has found herself in Wonderland.

CASE 55 SOLUTION

The man was Harry Houdini, who leapt into the river as part of his performance.

CASE 56 SOLUTION

The woman is Shakespeare's Lady Macbeth. She is trying to wash (imagined) blood from her hands.

CASE 57 SOLUTION

No one objects because the lady is a bottle of Mrs. Butterworth's™ syrup.

CASE 58 SOLUTION

The father is an emperor penguin, living in Antarctica.

CASE 59 SOLUTION

The star is Kermit the Frog and his girlfriend is Miss Piggy.

CASE 60 SOLUTION

The bald man is Howie Mandel. The man won $1 million on Deal or No Deal®.

CASE 61 SOLUTION

Marvin is bitten by mosquitoes that stay away after he applies insect repellant.

CASE 62 SOLUTION

The man is Stevie Wonder; he's singing and playing the piano.

CASE 63 SOLUTION

Winnie the Pooh lives in the Hundred Acre Wood.

CASE 64 SOLUTION

The children are Hansel and Gretel.

CASE 65 SOLUTION

Joan of Arc lived in France.

CASE 66 SOLUTION

Betsy Ross created the first American flag.

CASE 67 SOLUTION

Stevie is a snowman and he melted.

CASE 68 SOLUTION

Harriet Tubman is famous for helping to free slaves on the Underground Railroad before the American Civil War.

CASE 69 SOLUTION

The man is a TV news reporter; Vera turned off the TV with the remote control.

CASE 70 SOLUTION

He's a postman and is delivering/picking up mail.

CASE 71 SOLUTION

The son is Dumbo, an elephant born with enormous ears. The ears give him the ability to fly.

CASE 72 SOLUTION

Megan is taking a college entrance exam at her high school.

CASE 73 SOLUTION

Iraq and Kuwait were hit hardest by Operation Desert Storm in 1991.

CASE 74 SOLUTION

The man was scuba diving. He inflated his vest, ascended too quickly and died of the bends (too much nitrogen in the blood).

CASE 75 SOLUTION

The attending surgeon is Dr. Griffith's wife, also called Dr. Griffith, who can't operate on her own child.

CASE 76 SOLUTION

Butch works for a library; people are taking books.

CASE 77 SOLUTION

The man was skiing and fell off a ski lift.

CASE 78 SOLUTION

Stan is a priest. He works in a church.

CASE 79 SOLUTION

The ship is a submarine and none of the crew members were killed.

CASE 80 SOLUTION

The vehicle cleans the ice at ice hockey games.

CASE 81 SOLUTION

Nancy is looking for truffles, a delicacy prized by gourmands and chefs around the world.

CASE 82 SOLUTION

The man tried to join the U.S. Army in 1969.

CASE 83 SOLUTION

The son is Peter Rabbit and he steals Mr. McGregor's vegetables.

CASE 84 SOLUTION

Snow White survived the poisoning by getting a kiss from Prince Charming.

CASE 85 SOLUTION

The lab is a darkroom run by Wilma's ex-boss, who is a photographer.

CASE 86 SOLUTION

Kim is a pilot who works for an airline.

CASE 87 SOLUTION

They are the Blue Angels, airplanes from the U.S. Navy flight team; they travel to air shows around the globe.

CASE 88 SOLUTION

The island is Gilligan's Island and seven people survived.

CASE 89 SOLUTION

Johann Gutenberg printed a Bible in the 15th century.

CASE 90 SOLUTION

Jack is a shoe designer. His shoes support people by protecting their feet!

CASE 91 SOLUTION

The experts are animators and the rodent is Mickey Mouse®.

CASE 92 SOLUTION

Benjamin is a fire-eater. He uses the matches to light the torches that he puts into his mouth.

CASE 93 SOLUTION

The masked man is a hockey goalie who is attacked for 20 minutes in the first period.

CASE 94 SOLUTION

Maria is a tightrope walker at the circus.

CASE 95 SOLUTION

Star Trek®'s Enterprise uses lithium crystals as fuel.

CASE 96 SOLUTION

The man always wears yellow; the animal's name is Curious George.

CASE 97 SOLUTION

The creature is Big Bird as a balloon float. It can be found at Macy®'s Thanksgiving Day Parade in New York City.

CASE 98 SOLUTION

The man was a Union soldier who returned to his home when the Civil War ended in 1865.

CASE 99 SOLUTION

She's a professional racecar driver who loves circling the track.

CASE 100 SOLUTION

Thomas Jefferson and John Adams were U.S. presidents who both died on July 4, 1826.

CASE 101 SOLUTION

The man bought Newman's Own® Popcorn, Pasta Sauce, and Salad Dressing.

CASE 102 SOLUTION

Michelle is a figure skater competing for an Olympic gold medal.

CASE 103 SOLUTION

Danielle is a food stylist. She makes food look good so that it can be photographed.

CASE 104 SOLUTION

The man tells her to slow down; his radar gun clocked her speed.

CASE 105 SOLUTION

They heard a cat meowing and found it walled in with the body of Angela's father.

CASE 106 SOLUTION

The old lady swallowed a fly and died after swallowing a horse.

CASE 107 SOLUTION

Moss drove in Indiana in May at the Indianapolis 500.

CASE 108 SOLUTION

The man works as a rodeo clown who tries to distract the bull from the fallen rider.

CASE 109 SOLUTION

The man (Chuck Yeager) broke the sound barrier in an airplane.

CASE 110 SOLUTION

He is Uncle Sam, the image of patriotism, particularly during wartime.

CASE 111 SOLUTION

The crowd is watching Apolo Anton Ohno win the silver medal in the 1,000-meter speed skating race at the 2002 Winter Olympics in Park City, Utah.

CASE 112 SOLUTION

The bet took place in the late 19th century and led to the invention of the first motion picture.

CASE 113 SOLUTION

Jay had Brooke's email address and his computer crashed. It was no one's fault.

CASE 114 SOLUTION

The doctor has a dental degree (DDS) and removed Jason's wisdom teeth.

CASE 115 SOLUTION

Sara is a tollbooth collector and her clients are drivers.

CASE 116 SOLUTION

The murder weapon is a baseball bat and Detective Cracraft noticed that only one suspect is left-handed.

CASE 117 SOLUTION

The group is the Internal Revenue Service, which was founded in the 18th century.

CASE 118 SOLUTION

Rob and his neighbors heard their apartment's fire alarm; they're waiting to be sure that it was only a false alarm.

CASE 119 SOLUTION

They are driving the famous Route 66 highway that used to stretch all the way from Chicago to L.A.

CASE 120 SOLUTION

Chris is a professional poker player living in Las Vegas.

CASE 121 SOLUTION

Tom is a butcher working in a butcher shop.

CASE 122 SOLUTION

The man is looking at the Mona Lisa in Paris.

CASE 123 SOLUTION

A traffic light.

CASE 124 SOLUTION

Peter is a CSI investigator.

CASE 125 SOLUTION

The man is a crossing guard who uses a stop sign to control traffic.

CASE 126 SOLUTION

Sherry dropped her clothing off at her dry cleaner.

CASE 127 SOLUTION

The woman is the man's psychiatrist; she wrote him a prescription for anti-depressants.

CASE 128 SOLUTION

Peter is Peter Parker and he spends his nights fighting crime as Spider-Man.

CASE 129 SOLUTION

Bernadette is in a knitting class. The sharp objects are knitting needles and the binding material is yarn.

CASE 130 SOLUTION

The woman is a bike messenger; she can be found cycling around any metropolitan area.

CASE 131 SOLUTION

Steve is wearing a wireless headset; he is talking on his mobile phone.

CASE 132 SOLUTION

The animal's name is Toto and the road ends at the Emerald City.

CASE 133 SOLUTION

The paintings are ancient cave paintings.

CASE 134 SOLUTION

Gavin uses a computer to hack into banks' computer systems.

CASE 135 SOLUTION

The package contains Pop Rocks® candy, which explodes harmlessly when eaten.

CASE 136 SOLUTION

The product is a Post-It® Note, invented by Art Fry.

CASE 137 SOLUTION

Bob's full name is SpongeBob SquarePants.

CASE 138 SOLUTION

The man is a bartender and he made a martini.

CASE 139 SOLUTION

It's Sunday (and Daylight Savings Time has just begun).

CASE 140 SOLUTION

The animals are deer, which cause car accidents that kill approximately 100 people each year.

CASE 141 SOLUTION

The animal is a piñata pummeled by children at a birthday party.

CASE 142 SOLUTION

She is in a batting cage, hitting baseballs and practicing her swing.

CASE 143 SOLUTION

The men were astronauts on the moon.

CASE 144 SOLUTION

David was trampled during the running of the bulls in Pamplona, Spain.

CASE 145 SOLUTION

Mr. Blaine's business, Rick's Café, is located in Morocco.

CASE 146 SOLUTION

The Harlem Globetrotters® play basketball.

CASE 147 SOLUTION

They are in Yellowstone National Park, looking at the Old Faithful geyser.

CASE 148 SOLUTION

It's New Year's Eve and the man is in New York City's Times Square waiting for midnight.

CASE 149 SOLUTION

The people are archaeologists working in Egypt. (They uncovered a mummy.)

CASE 150 SOLUTION

The sign is in Los Angeles and it says "Hollywood."

CASE 151 SOLUTION

The man died of heat exhaustion in Death Valley.

CASE 152 SOLUTION

George is at a spa having a mud bath.

CASE 153 SOLUTION

The man is a butcher; he disposes of his victims in the dumpster behind his meat market.

CASE 154 SOLUTION

It is the Alamo in San Antonio, Texas.

CASE 155 SOLUTION

The people are in a movie theater and Vito is a theater usher.

CASE 156 SOLUTION

She is in a salon, getting a pedicure from trained pedicurists.

CASE 157 SOLUTION

The woman is the Statue of Liberty and she lives on New York City's Liberty Island.

CASE 158 SOLUTION

Dorothy is at a golf tournament. People aren't worried because Dorothy is hitting a golf ball, which is also known as "driving."

CASE 159 SOLUTION

The man lives in an igloo in Alaska.

CASE 160 SOLUTION

Two teams of kids are playing dodgeball in the school gymnasium.

CASE 161 SOLUTION

The creature is spotted at Universal Studios®; it is a mechanical shark from Jaws®.

CASE 162 SOLUTION

(Big) Ben tells time in London.

CASE 163 SOLUTION

The horses are Coney Island carousel horses.

CASE 164 SOLUTION

Nina is on the catwalk at a fashion show. She is a model.

CASE 165 SOLUTION

Jim resides in Paris, his last name is Morrison.

CASE 166 SOLUTION

The Great Wall of China was built in China and is a wall.

CASE 167 SOLUTION

The man is on Alcatraz. He feels trapped because he's a prisoner with a life sentence!

CASE 168 SOLUTION

The Trojan Horse was unleashed on the city of Troy.

CASE 169 SOLUTION

The girl is at the dentist. She pays the woman for services rendered.

CASE 170 SOLUTION

The group was camping in Tanzania atop Mount Kilimanjaro.

CASE 171 SOLUTION

The man is a vampire who lives in Transylvania and drinks blood.

CASE 172 SOLUTION

The place is Yosemite National Park in California; President Abraham Lincoln helped preserve it for future generations.

CASE 173 SOLUTION

Kai and Trevor are at a playground where Kai gets stuck at the top of the see-saw because he's much lighter than Trevor.

CASE 174 SOLUTION

Christopher has taken a trip to the Vatican. John is Pope John Paul II.

CASE 175 SOLUTION

The woman's husband was President John F. Kennedy; the couple was visiting Dallas, Texas.

CASE 176 SOLUTION

The woman died in the San Francisco earthquake; her body was covered by rubble for five days.

CASE 177 SOLUTION

The bar is in Alaska. The owner never has to give away any beer because the sun never sets there during the summer months.

CASE 178 SOLUTION

The men are Washington, Jefferson, Lincoln, and Roosevelt; they can be seen together at Mount Rushmore.

CASE 179 SOLUTION

The woman was convicted of witchcraft in Salem, Massachusetts.

CASE 180 SOLUTION

Cristina and her colleagues are inspecting a ship that sunk to the ocean floor; their deep-sea diving equipment prevents them from talking.

CASE 181 SOLUTION

The man is the girl's new bus driver. He is taking them home from school.

CASE 182 SOLUTION

The couple were in a roller coaster car at Walt Disney World®.

CASE 183 SOLUTION

The person is a journalist in Vietnam.

CASE 184 SOLUTION

Casey is in prison and Louis (her husband) is visiting her.

CASE 185 SOLUTION

Julio lives in Washington D.C.; Maryland and Virginia are the closest states to his home.

CASE 186 SOLUTION

Isabel is a disc jockey. She is in a room at a radio station where she's hosting her late-night radio show.

CASE 187 SOLUTION

Joseph left Russia; his birthday is one day away. (He crossed the International Date Line.)

CASE 188 SOLUTION

Lydia is a police officer heading toward Hughes Bank.

CASE 189 SOLUTION

Melissa is at an airport, waiting to catch a plane.

CASE 190 SOLUTION

The Olympic Torch was on its way to Atlanta.

CASE 191 SOLUTION

The woman had a hang glider and landed on the beach.

CASE 192 SOLUTION

The boy is on an airplane. The woman is a flight attendant.

CASE 193 SOLUTION

The man is Fidel Castro and he is the leader of Cuba.

CASE 194 SOLUTION

The boy is in McDonald®'s and he purchased a Happy Meal®.

CASE 195 SOLUTION

Georgia works in a bakery. She thanks the truck drivers for their business.

CASE 196 SOLUTION

The couple is getting married in a synagogue; in keeping with Jewish tradition, the new husband breaks a glass at the end of the ceremony.

CASE 197 SOLUTION

Leslie attends Tulane University, which was devastated by Hurricane Katrina in 2006. The university was closed while New Orleans recovered from the devastation, so students attended schools in other states.

CASE 198 SOLUTION

Monica is at a baseball game. The crowd sings "Take Me Out to the Ball Game."

CASE 199 SOLUTION

The woman works in a bar as a bartender.

CASE 200 SOLUTION

Sam spends his days in his barbershop. His "victims" are happy with the haircuts he gives them.

CASE 201 SOLUTION

The group is rafting down the Colorado River in the Grand Canyon.

CASE 202 SOLUTION

The village is the Lost Colony of Roanoke, located on Roanoke Island in North Carolina.

CASE 203 SOLUTION

Pierre is in Copenhagen, where the famous "Little Mermaid" statue sits by the bay.

CASE 204 SOLUTION

The man is in Fenway Park. His name is Daniel Ortiz and he is a Designated Hitter for the Boston Red Sox. The crowd erupts in thunderous applause when he hits a home run over the left field wall, or "Green Monster."

CASE 205 SOLUTION

The man is having his car parked in a garage; he retrieves his car after work.

CASE 206 SOLUTION

Steve and Eve are at a boxing match. The "predator" leaves after winning the bout.

CASE 207 SOLUTION

She can be found in a concert hall, conducting an orchestra.

CASE 208 SOLUTION

Mr. Smith is a crossing guard at the local school.

CASE 209 SOLUTION

Max fell asleep on the beach and his clothes floated away.

CASE 210 SOLUTION

Chuck works as a nurse at the local hospital.

CASE 211 SOLUTION

The authorities found the wife's gold wedding ring at the bottom of the vat. George's plan failed because gold only dissolves in aqua regia (a mixture of sulfuric and nitric acids).

CASE 212 SOLUTION

In February 2002, the New England Patriots football team defeated the St. Louis Rams in Super Bowl XXXVI, which was held in New Orleans.

CASE 213 SOLUTION

The river is frozen.

CASE 214 SOLUTION

Connie taped the game earlier in the day and had already watched the end when she sat down to watch it with her family.

CASE 215 SOLUTION

The woman is blind and was reading a book in Braille.

CASE 216 SOLUTION

Courtney and Mike ordered sushi.

CASE 217 SOLUTION

Mel is a "leg" model, but the cuts were not on her legs.

CASE 218 SOLUTION

The creature is a human being. It is dangerous because it sometimes does not use its intelligence well.

CASE 219 SOLUTION

Herbie lives in Australia, where July is a winter month.

CASE 220 SOLUTION

The women are in a self-defense class and attack the man as part of their training.

CASE 221 SOLUTION

It was Dolly the sheep, the first cloned mammal.

CASE 222 SOLUTION

Barbara is stationed on a submarine.

CASE 223 SOLUTION

The doctor is ordering his breakfast from a waitress at the hospital cafeteria.

CASE 224 SOLUTION

Fred isn't allergic to his mouse because it's a computer mouse. He keeps it next to his computer.

CASE 225 SOLUTION

The man drowned and his body washed out to sea.

CASE 226 SOLUTION

Bob is playing 30 Second Mysteries.

CASE 227 SOLUTION

Jack was playing a video game.

CASE 228 SOLUTION

The official works for the Department of Motor Vehicles; Jill is smiling because she just passed her driving test.

CASE 229 SOLUTION

The people are children in Halloween costumes who say "Trick-or-treat!"

CASE 230 SOLUTION

Zack is having a garage sale.

CASE 231 SOLUTION

*The substance does not kill Ed because it is just a cup of coffee.
He drinks it first thing in the morning.*

CASE 232 SOLUTION

*The young man is a war photographer who bravely goes into battle to
shoot pictures of soldiers at war.*

CASE 233 SOLUTION

Jane is deaf.

CASE 234 SOLUTION

The woman is Margaret's mother; Margaret was punished because she drew on the wall.

CASE 235 SOLUTION

Chip is a dog who competes in dog races.

CASE 236 SOLUTION

They are at an imaginary tea party and Rose is a doll that is placed in a playroom.

CASE 237 SOLUTION

Lucy is a dog. A veterinary surgeon operates on her.

CASE 238 SOLUTION

An ace captures the king; no one is injured because war is just a card game!

CASE 239 SOLUTION

The woman is in Las Vegas and needs change to play the slot machines.

CASE 240 SOLUTION

The photographers are in the White House Rose Garden to take pictures of George W. Bush and family.

CASE 241 SOLUTION

The ice in the drinks was poisoned; George drank his iced tea before the ice melted.

CASE 242 SOLUTION

The man died of hypothermia and couldn't swim because the lake was covered with ice.

CASE 243 SOLUTION

Jules was drinking soda, but he was only 15 years old and didn't know how to drive.

CASE 244 SOLUTION

The foreign world is Legoland®. The family stays because they are on vacation.

CASE 245 SOLUTION

The woman jumped out of a plane. The children didn't help because she had a parachute.

CASE 246 SOLUTION

It is a graduation ceremony and the graduates will throw their caps into the air.

CASE 247 SOLUTION

Julia is a boa constrictor in a zoo. Sometimes snakes will go long periods of time without eating.

CASE 248 SOLUTION

The people are playing Clue®. They identify the murderer using the clues provided in the game.

CASE 249 SOLUTION

Sue is an ice sculptor; her sculptures melt.

CASE 250 SOLUTION

Sally isn't afraid because the voice is on her answering machine. Her dad is letting her know that they are coming home to pick her up.

CASE 251 SOLUTION

The man is on vacation where the temperature is 20° Celsius.

CASE 252 SOLUTION

Dr. Cooper passed out because he was given anesthesia; he can operate now that he is recovered from his surgery.

CASE 253 SOLUTION

Ursula was not in the car; she was talking to Bob on his cell phone.

CASE 254 SOLUTION

All three people are on treadmills in a gym.

CASE 255 SOLUTION

The men are movers and the family found their belongings in their new house.

CASE 256 SOLUTION

The woman is "Madison" from the movie Splash. She is afraid because she turns into a mermaid in water.

CASE 257 SOLUTION

Toni is a meter maid; she's disliked because she writes people parking tickets.

CASE 258 SOLUTION

The man is a stuntman, who crashed the car for a movie scene.

CASE 259 SOLUTION

The parents leave the room because Barney bores them.

CASE 260 SOLUTION

*Jenny isn't worried because the mouse is for her computer.
It was misplaced during the move.*

CASE 261 SOLUTION

Jim won the Belmont Stakes. His killer was a veterinarian.

CASE 262 SOLUTION

Andy was at the school to vote in an election.

CASE 263 SOLUTION

The hotel management is nice to Tami because they want to impress her. She is a journalist who reviews hotels.

CASE 264 SOLUTION

The man is a starter in the Olympics and the women ran 100 meters.

CASE 265 SOLUTION

Alvin is attacked by a fit of sneezing; he can continue driving because sneezing is quick and practically harmless.

CASE 266 SOLUTION

Peter carries pictures because they are printed on money, which he gives away when he buys things.

CASE 267 SOLUTION

Alexandra is a licensed acupuncturist; her patients sometimes bleed because they are being stuck with needles.

CASE 268 SOLUTION

The crowd has gathered to watch a parade; they run for cover because it starts to rain.

CASE 269 SOLUTION

The diver was already dead when his oxygen ran out and his body floated up to the surface.

CASE 270 SOLUTION

Bob is a bus driver; the customers leave when they reach their stops.

CASE 271 SOLUTION

It's October and Jensen is a pitcher in the American League playing in the World Series.

CASE 272 SOLUTION

She is Madeline, the star and namesake of the series of children's books by Ludwig Bemelmans.

CASE 273 SOLUTION

The boy is Josh from the movie Big. Josh's mother screamed because he turned into a 30-year-old man. He ran away to New York City.

CASE 274 SOLUTION

The men are security guards who are driving an armored car.

CASE 275 SOLUTION

He is a midget (or little person) and he cannot reach the button for the top floor. On rainy days, he can use his umbrella to press the button.

CASE 276 SOLUTION

Mary is a sculptor who "painted" her face with makeup in preparation for her show. She is happy that people notice her sculptures instead of her face.

CASE 277 SOLUTION

Candy is a judge presiding over a trial.

CASE 278 SOLUTION

Lulu ate gummi worms®. She didn't get sick because they're an edible treat!

CASE 279 SOLUTION

Nina is playing Monopoly® and landed on the square that says "Go to Jail." She could spend up to three turns there.

CASE 280 SOLUTION

Two players just sat down to play Battleship®; there will be no fatalities in this "war" because it's only a game.